OUTMARKET

THE

COMPETITION

Advanced Marketing Tactics
to Drive Growth and Profitability

NICK DOYLE

**FAST
COMPANY**
Press

Published by Fast Company Press
New York, New York
www.fastcompanypress.com

Distributed by Greenleaf Book Group

For ordering information or special discounts for bulk purchases, please contact Greenleaf Book Group at PO Box 91869, Austin, TX 78709, 512.891.6100.

Design and composition by Greenleaf Book Group and Chase Quarterman
Cover design by Greenleaf Book Group and Chase Quarterman

For permission to reproduce copyrighted material, grateful acknowledgment is made to the following:
Arthur J. Gallagher Risk Management Services, LLC from figures 4.4, 4.5, 4.6, 4.7, 4.8, 4.9, 6.2, 6.3, 7.2, and 7.3. Copyright © 2024. All rights reserved. Certain trademarks, service marks and copyrights referenced herein are used under limited license by Arthur J. Gallagher Risk Management Services, LLC. All other trademarks, service marks, and copyrights are property of the respective owners.

Harvard Business Review from "If Brands Are Built Over Years, Why Are They Managed Over Quarters?" by Leonard M. Lodish and Carl F. Mela. Copyright © 2007 *Harvard Business Review*, July–August 2007.

Harvard Business Review from "The Right Way to Build Your Brand" by Roger L. Martin, Jann Schwarz, and Mimi Turner. Copyright © 2024 *Harvard Business Review*, January–February 2024.

Tzvika Barenholz from "The Trouble with Green Dashboards" by Tzvika Barenholz. Copyright © 2020 by the author, Medium.com, 4 September 2020.

Publisher's Cataloging-in-Publication data is available.

Print ISBN: 978-1-63908-103-5

eBook ISBN: 978-1-63908-104-2

To offset the number of trees consumed in the printing of our books, Greenleaf donates a portion of the proceeds from each printing to the Arbor Day Foundation. Greenleaf Book Group has replaced over 50,000 trees since 2007.

Printed in the United States of America on acid-free paper

25 26 27 28 29 30 31   10 9 8 7 6 5 4 3 2 1

First Edition

To my father, Joe Doyle,
who taught me what it means to be "The Man in the Arena"
and to whom I owe my passion for this subject

CONTENTS

GLOSSARY

In this glossary, you'll find definitions of key terms and concepts that are used throughout this book. These terms have been carefully selected to enhance your understanding of the material and to provide clarity on specialized language that may be unfamiliar or used in a specific context. By providing a dedicated glossary for these terms (and placing it in the front of the book), we aim to ensure you have a quick and easy reference point as you navigate through the chapters.

You will notice that some terms in the book are **highlighted** for emphasis. These highlighted terms represent important concepts that are critical to grasping the core ideas being discussed.

Hopefully this glossary serves as a helpful resource to deepen your comprehension and make the most of the insights shared in this book.

4 Ps–A framework created by Neil Borden and E. Jerome McCarthy that catalogs product marketing levers. These levers can be adjusted to improve positioning and influence customers. In advanced marketing, each of these is thoughtfully considered and iterated upon. The 4 Ps are:

1. Product—what you're selling

2. Price—what your product costs

3. Place—where your product is sold

4. Promotion—how your product is advertised

A/B Test or Multivariate Testing–An evaluation to determine which of two, or more if multivariate, assets performs best in the marketplace. Assets might include promotions, ads, content, copy, etc.

Marketers run multiple versions of the promotion or asset simultaneously, randomly determining which will cause users to take the desired action. Once testers acquire a critical mass of data, they determine a winner.

Beware of either/or thinking: sometimes assets can have different strengths. For that reason, it's important to be thoughtful about what you measure and how.

Abandoned Cart Retargeting–A method for re-engaging e-commerce shoppers after they place items in their carts, then navigate away without purchasing. These shoppers are usually among your highest-value leads. You'll likely want to retarget with an urgent cadence, and you may also want to provide additional incentives to return.

ABM–See "Account-Based Marketing"

Account-Based Marketing–A method of B2B marketing in which you select a few, high-value organizations (or "accounts") to target directly. In certain cases, this can be more effective than a traditional wide-net targeting approach like inbound marketing, where you may end up spending resources on many low-value or low-intent leads.

Acquisition–(1) The process of moving prospects down the funnel, from making impressions to generating leads and finally converting them into customers.

(2) The funnel phase in which you make your first impression and encourage targets to enter the funnel, becoming leads.

Note that, due to the breadth of the first definition, the term "acquisition" is used for two different allowables. The customer acquisition cost (CAC) allowable governs the entire process of gathering impressions and shepherding them through the funnel to conversion. Meanwhile, the cost per acquisition (CPA) allowable specifically governs conversion.

See the "Lifetime Value Framework Allowables" cheat sheet
See "Conversion"

AI–See "Artificial Intelligence"

Allowable–A campaign financing metric, measuring the maximum amount that one might spend in a given campaign. Note that while this term technically refers to a maximum number, it is usually best to spend an amount equal to or just below your allowable. If you spend significantly less than your allowable, you will miss opportunities, effectively leaving money on the table.

For other metrics, see "Performance Metrics" and "Projection Metrics."

For a list of allowables in the Lifetime Value Framework, see the "Lifetime Value Framework Allowables" cheat sheet.

Anchoring–The exploitation of a cognitive bias in which consumers judge value based on the first option they were presented with (the "anchor"). Retailers use anchoring all the time, overpricing a product, then putting it "on sale." The concept of anchoring was first introduced in 1974, by Daniel Kahneman and Amos Tversky in *Thinking Fast and Slow.*

Artificial Intelligence–Technologies that simulate human intelligence, including technologies built with machine learning and/or logic-based algorithms. AIs can write copy, analyze data, and even bid on PPC ads. Today, marketers use AI software to accelerate and augment their work, create content, optimize performance, and automate operations. AI makes it possible to spend less while doing more, faster.

See the "Five-Tactic Marketing Framework" cheat sheet

Attribution/Attribution Models–The evaluation of campaign touchpoints, determining how much each contributes to outcomes like lead generation or conversion. In a multi-channel campaign, attribution is essential for determining which channels and touchpoints deliver the most value. Ultimately, these determinations will help you optimize spending and maximize results.

There are a number of popular attribution models. For examples, see

"First Click Attribution," "Last Click Attribution," "Linear Attribution," "Position-Based Attribution," and "Time Decay Attribution."

Average Net Margin–A profitability metric, expressing what percentage of your total revenue is net profit. To calculate it, divide average net profit by average total revenue. Ultimately, your average net margin will be useful for calculating your customer acquisition cost allowable. (See the "Lifetime Value Framework Allowables" cheat sheet.)

Awareness Stage–The first stage of the buyer's journey and the very top of the funnel. This is when prospects first learn about your company, product, or service. During this stage, the most important framework tactic is brand marketing.

See "Buyer's Journey"

B2B–An acronym for "business-to-business," contrasted with B2C ("business-to-consumer"). B2Bs sell to other businesses, rather than directly to consumers. B2Bs generally have fewer customers, greater transaction values, larger order sizes, and more stakeholders per transaction. Consequently, B2B and B2C strategies sometimes differ. While many of this book's recommendations apply across all marketing domains, our particular focus is on B2B.

See "B2C"

B2C–An acronym for "business-to-consumer," contrasted with B2B ("business-to-business"). B2Cs sell directly to consumers, rather than to other businesses. They generally have lower transaction values and greater transaction volumes. Their targets often make buying decisions quickly, based on personal preference, with very few stakeholders. And, unlike most B2Bs, many B2Cs transact business in retail stores. Consequently, B2B and B2C strategies sometimes differ. While many of this book's recommendations apply across all marketing domains, our particular focus is on B2B.

See "B2B"

Backlinks–Links to your website, found on other websites. Search engines like Google consider valid backlinks to be votes of confidence, demonstrating the popularity and authority of your site. Those votes are weighted based on the quality of the website that backlinks to you. (A reputable news site will carry more sway than a spammy blog.) Ultimately, earning backlinks from reputable sources will help you get to the top of Google's search results.

See "Search Engine Optimization"

BDRs–See "Business Development Representatives"

Brand Marketing – Brand marketing promotes a brand's unique identity without necessarily delivering a direct call to action. It's designed to increase the likelihood that someone will think of you and your product first when they are ready to buy. Brand marketing also promotes trust and positive emotional associations with your business, which can deepen customer loyalty, reduce price sensitivity, and boost the impact of performance marketing campaigns.

See "Mental Availability"

See "Share of Voice"

See the "Five-Tactic Marketing Framework" cheat sheet

Brand Response Ads–Ads that combine strategies from both brand marketing and performance marketing. These ads can be effective, although both the brand and performance effects are usually weaker than with ads that specifically target one individual type: brand or performance. A famous example would be GEICO's creative TV commercials with their ubiquitous "Fifteen minutes could save you 15% or more" tagline.

See "Brand Marketing" and "Performance Marketing"

Brand Value–A monetary estimation of your brand's worth, accounting for factors like trust, mental availability, and affinity versus a commodity brand.

See "Brand Marketing"

Burn Pixel–An invisible, pixel-sized image that's embedded in digital assets like ads and web pages. You can track who sees these pixels, when, and where. Then you can use this data to guide your retargeting efforts. For example, burn pixels can help you avoid exposing users to the same ad repeatedly, or they can help you track where users are in a sequential messaging campaign. You may also want a burn pixel on your purchase confirmation page, helping ensure that you don't inadvertently retarget customers after conversion.

See "Remarketing"

See "Retargeting"

Business Development Representatives–Sales reps who focus on generating leads and developing new business opportunities. Whereas other sales reps focus on conversion, BDRs focus on the top of the funnel. They qualify leads from marketing campaigns, and independently prospect for new accounts, often following up with cold outreach and/or scheduled pitches.

Buyer's Journey–The path that a buyer takes from impression through conversion. You might think of the buyer's journey as the funnel from the buyer's perspective. It is the sales process as experienced from your prospect's perspective.

On their journey, buyers move through three stages.

1. Awareness—the buyer realizes that they need/want something.

2. Consideration—they research and compare options.

3. Decision—they decide whether to purchase.

Mapping out your buyer's journey will help you create the right marketing strategy for each stage.

Buying Indicators–Signals that a prospect may be ready to buy. Examples include requesting a quote, starting a chat, downloading case studies, scheduling a demo, and filling a cart.

CAC–See "Customer Acquisition Cost"

Call to Action–A marketing message that provokes an immediate response, such as "Call Now," "Learn More," "Free Shipping on orders over $XXX," "Buy one Get one Free," or "Subscribe Today." The purpose of a CTA is to convert passive targets into active ones. CTAs are a central feature of performance marketing.

See "Performance Marketing"

Campaign–A coordinated marketing effort with a single, unified objective. For example, a campaign may be built to sell a product, attract subscribers, boost attendance, or even promote an idea. Note that a single campaign can incorporate many assets (ads, emails, landing pages, etc.), channels (print, digital, experiential, etc.), and strategies (brand marketing, performance marketing, content marketing, etc.).

See "Integrated Campaigns"

Campaign Half-Life–The time it takes for a campaign's effectiveness to diminish by half. This metric is used to measure the resonance or response rate of a campaign. Measuring half-life also enables you to evaluate campaign outcomes faster: you can judge the efficacy of the campaign when you reach your halfway point, rather than waiting for complete results.

Campaign half-life generally follows a long-tail curve: returns spike at the beginning of your campaign, drop dramatically, then slowly fade out over a broader span of time. Half-life will be different based on different types of campaigns. For example, TV and radio historically have had a half-life of 24 hours depending on the campaign type. By contrast, direct mail historically has had a half-life of 10 days from in-home date.

CCPA–The California Consumer Privacy Act regulates how companies handle consumer data. Any business that sells to California residents must comply. Because of the CCPA and other regulations, third-party data may soon become less useful. It's also important to note that while gating content is great for collecting data on prospects, collecting that additional data may also make it more difficult to comply with the CCPA.

See "GDPR"

Channel–A messaging medium or platform used by marketers. Example channels include social media, organic search, direct mail, TV, radio, paid search, etc.

No two channels are alike: channels often communicate in different ways, incur different costs, and reach different audiences—at different times, in different places. For this reason, it's important that every marketing campaign take a multi-channel approach.

See "Multi-Channel Campaigns"

See "Incremental Lift"

See "Integrated Campaigns"

Clickthrough Rate–A metric for evaluating the performance of ads, emails, and other kinds of digital marketing content. CTR measures how often viewers of your content actually clicked on it, ostensibly illustrating how effective that content was. But beware: CTR figures can be deceiving. The ad with the highest clickthrough rate may not yield the most purchases. And ads with lower CTRs may still be useful for reaching otherwise-neglected audiences.

You can think of CTR as the ratio of clicks to views. To calculate it, divide the number of clicks by the number of times your ad was shown. The higher the ratio, the better the performance.

CLV–See "Customer Lifetime Value"

Confidence Interval–A statistical figure indicating how reliable your metrics are. Confidence intervals tell you whether your data is generating genuine insight or mere speculation. In cases where confidence is low, calculating your interval can save you from taking your metrics too seriously. For example, running an A/B test on 20 people might give you a definitive result, but you shouldn't take that result seriously: 20 responses isn't a statistically significant data set. In a case like this one, the confidence interval will drop dramatically, signaling to you that something's wrong with your data.

See "A/B Test"

Consideration Stage–The middle phase of the buyer's journey, after your prospect has developed an interest, but before they've decided whether to purchase. During the consideration stage, buyers research and compare options. As they move through this stage, buyers will narrow their choices, seek out new information, and wrestle with the cost of buying.

See "Buyer's Journey"

Content Marketing–A marketing strategy that emphasizes the ad's information over its promotion. Common media channels include books, blogs, videos, brochures, and social media posts.

Rather than advertise brands or deliver sales pitches, successful content marketing educates prospects about relevant products and services. Ultimately, this educational material stimulates interest and builds trust among prospects. Content can also be used to generate leads, either offering educational materials in exchange for prospect data, or else hyperlinking to lead-capture forms and campaigns.

Note that content marketing requires lots of lead time, taking months or even years to begin enhancing overall performance. On the plus side, good content evergreens will pay off for years.

See "Inbound Marketing"

Conversion–

1. Turning a lead into a customer (i.e., closing a sale)

2. The funnel phase during which leads convert into customers. The key allowables during this phase are customer acquisition cost and cost per acquisition.

Conversion Rate–See "Customer Conversion Rate"

Conversion Rate Optimization–The systematic process for increasing purchase rates among site visitors. To optimize conversion, marketers identify friction points in the sales process (for instance, determining when most lost prospects abandon the cart). Then they incrementally address these points of friction. They may reconsider aesthetic components like layout, design, wording, and messaging cadence. They may also want to rethink monetary incentives, exploring potential offers and financing options.

With proper analysis, CRO can improve your conversion results by 50–100%+, reducing your cost per acquisition while increasing your available pool of funds (your allowable customer acquisition cost).

Cost per Acquisition–The fifth and final metric of the Lifetime Value Framework. CPA expresses how much it costs to convert leads into customers. More specifically, there are three kinds of CPA metrics:

1. CPA performance—the current, actual cost of converting leads to customers

2. CPA allowable—the maximum or ideal amount that you should spend converting leads

3. CPA projection—the hypothetical cost of conversion under alternative conditions, calculated to inform campaign planning

See the "Lifetime Value Framework Allowables" cheat sheet

Cost per Click–

1. An efficiency metric, measuring how much you spend on advertising in order to earn a single click. This is calculated by dividing your total ad spend by the number of clicks you received.

2. The rate set by publishers who sell ad space using a pay per click model. Rate calculation is often automated and rises with your impression share.

See "Pay Per Click"

For an alternative efficiency metric, see "Cost per Thousand Impressions."

Cost per Lead—The fourth metric of the Lifetime Value Framework. CPL expresses how much it costs to generate each new lead. More specifically, there are three kinds of CPL metrics:

1. CPL performance—the current, actual cost of generating each new lead

2. CPL allowable—the maximum or ideal amount that you should spend generating a new lead

3. CPL projection—the hypothetical cost of lead generation under alternative conditions, calculated to inform campaign planning

See the "Lifetime Value Framework Allowables" cheat sheet

Cost per Thousand Impressions—The third metric of the Lifetime Value Framework. CPM (technically, "cost per mille" but stated as "cost per thousand") expresses how much it costs to generate a thousand new impressions. More specifically, there are three kinds of CPM metrics:

1. CPM performance—the current, actual cost of generating a thousand impressions

2. CPM allowable—the maximum or ideal amount that you should spend generating a thousand impressions

3. CPL projection—the hypothetical cost of generating impressions under alternative conditions, calculated to inform campaign planning

See the "Lifetime Value Framework Allowables" cheat sheet

CPA–See "Cost per Acquisition"

CPC–See "Cost per Click"

CPL–See "Cost per Lead"

CPM See "Cost per Thousand Impressions"

CRO–See "Conversion Rate Optimization"

Cross-Channel Attribution–See "Attribution/Attribution Models"

Cross-Selling–Selling related or complementary products to existing customers, post-conversion. Cross-selling is one of the most powerful things you can do to drive up Customer Lifetime Value, giving you more money to play with at every stage of the funnel. In this way, cross-selling is similar to the other two major post-conversion marketing efforts: upselling and promoting subscription renewals.
See "Renewal"
See "Upselling"
See "Post-Conversion"
See "Customer Lifetime Value"

CTA–See "Call to Action"

Customer Acquisition–See "Acquisition"

Customer Acquisition Cost–The second metric of the Lifetime Value Framework. CAC expresses the total cost of acquiring each new customer, from impression through conversion. More specifically, there are three kinds of CAC metrics:

1. CAC performance—the current, actual cost of acquiring each new customer

2. CAC allowable—the maximum or ideal amount that you should spend on marketing efforts across the entire funnel

3. CAC projection—the hypothetical cost of customer acquisition under alternative conditions, calculated to inform campaign planning

See the "Lifetime Value Framework Allowables" cheat sheet

Customer Conversion Rate—The key metric for evaluating performance in the conversion stage of the funnel. CCR measures the percentage of leads who ultimately convert by making a purchase. To calculate it, divide converted customers by leads generated.

Boosting your CCR will improve efficiency across the entire funnel: with a higher CCR, you can generate more revenue from fewer leads. And that new revenue can then be pumped back into your marketing efforts, generating more leads and further improving CCR.

Customer Experience—The overall impression of your company that customers get while interacting with you—from initial awareness through post-conversion. Contributing factors can include elements like product quality, messaging resonance, support team responsiveness, and UI and UX design.

In addition to improving sales, CX is key for growing customer lifetime value. It helps you deepen long-term customer loyalty and attract more post-conversion interactions like up-sales, cross-sales, and renewals. Ultimately, this enhanced lifetime value will increase capital for marketing efforts across the entire funnel.

See "Five Es of Customer Experience"

Customer Lifetime Value—The first metric of the Lifetime Value

Framework. CLV expresses how much total revenue the average customer will yield by the end of their relationship with your company. This metric is used as the basis for all other Lifetime Value calculations.

An increase in CLV will boost all of your allowable spending across the entire funnel. Raising CLV usually involves post-conversion engagements like upselling, cross-selling, and promoting renewals—as well as expanding and enhancing customer experience.

See the "Lifetime Value Framework Allowables" cheat sheet

See "Customer Experience"

See "Renewal"

See "Upselling"

See "Post-Conversion"

See "Customer Lifetime Value"

Customer Persona–A fictional profile of your ideal target buyer based on market research and existing customer data. In B2B, personas may also be used to profile influencers, stakeholders, and workplace decision-makers.

Personas commonly include features like demographic details, personal values, channel preferences, and buying patterns. In B2B, they'll likely capture job titles, job descriptions, and much more.

Personas are ultimately used to inform content creation and campaign strategies. Be sure that they reflect the actual results of research and data analysis—not merely assumptions or anecdotal experiences.

Customer Research–The process of identifying who your potential customers are and what makes them tick—their needs, preferences, behaviors, and motivations. Research approaches can include interviews, focus groups, surveys, and customer advisory panels.

In B2B, it can be helpful to begin with the firmographics of your existing customers: industry, geography, titles of decision-makers/influencers, how and where they buy, etc.

Customer Retention–

1. Your business's ability to maintain customer relationships post-conversion and generate more revenue from those relationships

2. A name for the funnel phase after conversion

Usually, when customer retention is high, each individual customer will yield more lifetime revenue. When customer retention is low, customer lifetime value usually drops, requiring you to convert more leads into customers.

The quality of your customer retention often correlates with the quality of your customer experience.

See "Customer Experience"
See "Renewal"
See "Upselling"
See "Post-Conversion"
See "Customer Lifetime Value"

Customer Segments/Segmentation–See "Segments/Segmentation"

CX–See "Customer Experience"

Data Puking–A term coined by analytics maven Avinash Kaushik. The fear that you don't have enough data can often lead to "data puking": the presentation of large swaths of data without thoughtful curation or meaningful insights. Here, data is collected and presented for its own sake and is not packaged or analyzed to inform business decisions.

Decoy Effect/Pricing–A phenomenon whereby buyer preference between two options changes when presented with a third "decoy" option. The decoy makes your preferred option seem more appealing by comparison, steering buyers in that direction.

More technically, the decoy is "asymmetrically dominated," which is to say that it is incontrovertibly worse than your target option but is a mixed tradeoff with respect to your lowest-tier option.

A common deployment of the decoy model is "good, better, best" pricing, with the better and best options priced more closely than the good option. This invariably leads to the better option being the most selected.

Direct Mail Campaigns–The delivery of hard copy advertising collateral via postal mail. This can include personalized letters, postcards, dimensional mailers, inserts, and physical samples.

Direct Method of Value Determination–When calculating allowables in the Lifetime Value Framework, the direct method draws on actual historic business data (aka "performance metrics") instead of drawing on projections. The result is an allowable that reflects how much capital is actually available to your business today.

This terminology is borrowed from accounting, where we similarly distinguish between the direct method of accounting (also called "cash basis") and the accrual method of accounting. The direct method of accounting records transactions when money changes hands, whereas accrual accounting records transactions when money is earned or expenses are incurred (usually at the time of invoicing).

See "Performance Metrics"
See "Projection Metrics"
See "Allowable"
See the "Lifetime Value Framework Allowables" cheat sheet

E-Com/E-Commerce–Short for "electronic commerce," e-commerce refers to the exchange of goods and services over the internet. This includes transactions conducted via websites, mobile apps, and virtual marketplaces.

ESOV–See "Extra Share of Voice"

Extra Share of Voice–A metric expressing how much your share of voice exceeds your share of market. Cultivating a high extra share of voice increases brand awareness, consideration, and purchase intent. Over time, this extra share of voice will generate more sales, improving your share of market.

A high ESOV reflects an aggressive, growth-oriented approach to marketing spending, where spending is disproportionately high relative to your current market position.

See "Share of Voice"

See "Share of Market"

See "Mental Availability"

Five Es of Customer Experience–A customer experience design framework advanced by Isaac Jeffries, mapping CX efforts to the buyer's voyage from initial impression through post-conversion. The Five Es articulate the five actions you must take at each stage of the voyage. High-quality customer experiences see intentional design at each stage.

1. Entice—attract interest in your brand

2. Enter—offer a first touchpoint for customer interaction

3. Engage—conduct business with your customer

4. Exit—end the transaction

5. Extend—encourage repeat business and a longer relationship

See "Customer Experience"

Fine-Tuning–Retraining an existing AI model to perform a more specific task. For example, training an existing AI chatbot to refer to your internal support wiki when responding to queries.

Fine-tuning is faster and more affordable than developing custom AI tools. It allows you to leverage pre-developed technology while customizing for your brand's specific needs and objectives.

First Click Attribution–An attribution model that assigns all of the credit for any given conversion to that customer's first interaction. Examples of first interactions might include ad clickthrough rates, website visits, and content downloads (such as ebooks).

This model shines a light on how customers enter your funnel, but it risks undervaluing other interactions at the consideration and conversion stages. Ultimately, first click may misrepresent what actually caused your customer to buy.

See "Attribution/Attribution Models"

First Interaction Attribution–See "First Click Attribution"

First-Party Data–Data collected directly by your company through interactions with customers and site visitors. Examples include contact information, transaction history, website activity, app usage, and survey responses.

First-party data tends to be more reliable and actionable than third-party data. As regulations tighten around third-party data, first-party data is becoming increasingly essential.

See "Second-Party Data"
See "Third-Party Data"

Framing–When presenting information, crafting the context in order to alter audience interpretation and response. First studied by psychologists Daniel Kahneman and Amos Tversky, framing exploits cognitive biases to improve impressions of product quality and price. Framing can raise conversion rates and other KPIs, but it's important to note that deceptive framing can also put customer trust at risk.

See "Anchoring"
See "Decoy Effect"

Funnel–A framework for visualizing the process of customer onboarding. The funnel illustrates how awareness and consideration translate to leads and how leads convert into long-term customer relationships. As prospects travel down the funnel, population size shrinks, but revenue potential per prospect grows.

There are many ways of breaking down the funnel. In this book, the funnel is broken into four stages:

1. Acquisition top—transforming impressions into prospects

2. Acquisition bottom—transforming prospects into leads

3. Conversion—transforming leads into customers

4. Post-conversion—extending customer relationships and boosting lifetime value

Managing budget allocation across funnel stages is crucial for efficient growth. That budgeting is done through the Lifetime Value Framework.

See "Acquisition"

See "Conversion"

See "Post-Conversion"

See the "Lifetime Value Framework Allowables" cheat sheet

Gated Content–Digital content that requires viewers to fill out a form with contact info before accessing. Examples include research reports, tip sheets, webinars, and premium articles.

Gated content exchanges value for data, allowing you to generate and qualify leads. But gated access also creates friction, decreasing total viewership. The tradeoff must be weighed carefully.

As privacy regulations tighten, the value of gated content may diminish.

See "Content Marketing"

GDPR–The General Data Protection Regulation regulates how companies handle consumer data when doing business with citizens of the EU. Any business that sells to EU citizens must comply, and fines for non-compliance can be steep. Because of the GDPR and other regulations, third-party data may soon become less useful. It's also important to note that while gating content is great for collecting data on prospects, collecting that additional data may also make it more difficult to comply with the GDPR.

See "CCPA"

Generative AI–Artificial intelligence software that rapidly creates brand-new digital content with minimal human involvement. Generative AI empowers you to elevate and accelerate marketing efforts, delivering results at lightning speed and low cost. Sample applications include:

- Campaign ideation

- Market research

- Collateral and content creation

- Customer persona development

- Web & app development

- Customer-facing support

Note that generative AI can deliver imperfect results, misrepresenting facts or offering sub-optimal solutions. It can also stray from brand values, legal/ethical standards, and customer expectations. For this reason, it's best to use these tools for first drafts and thought partnerships, tapping human contributors to review and revise the AI's output.

Geofencing–A technique for location-based digital marketing. Geofencing uses a mobile device's physical location to trigger marketing actions, drawing on data from GPS, RFID, Wi-Fi, and/or cellular. For instance, you might geofence to reach students at a particular university, exclusively delivering ads and other messaging to devices within the boundaries of that campus.

ICP–See "Ideal Customer Profile"

Ideal Customer Profile–A description of prospects more likely to deliver high customer lifetime value once acquired. For B2B, ICPs often include industry, size, tech stack, business model, and budget.

Defining an ICP helps you qualify leads and identify high-intent buying signals. It also informs overall segmentation, targeting, messaging, and positioning.

Impression–A single view or interaction with your marketing content. Examples include seeing an ad on a web page, opening an email, and spotting an outdoor billboard. Relative to other brand engagements, impressions are the broadest, occurring in the largest population and delivering the most general information.

While impressions do not directly translate to sales, they are crucial in two related domains:

1. Brand marketing—quality impressions raise awareness of your brand's unique identity and increase the likelihood that someone will think of you when they are ready to buy.

2. Acquisition top—the funnel's first phase, during which you reach out to a large audience, cultivating awareness.

Impression spending is governed by your cost per thousand impressions (CPM) allowable.

See "Acquisition"
See "Awareness Stage"
See "Brand Marketing"
See "Cost per Thousand Impressions"
See "Customer Persona"
See the "Lifetime Value Framework Allowables" cheat sheet

Impression Conversion Rate–A campaign efficiency metric, expressing how many impressions it takes to generate one lead. ICR is calculated by dividing your total conversions by your total impressions. For ICR, a variety of interactions may qualify as conversions, including website visits, content downloads, and lead form submissions.

A high ICR indicates that your messaging is well targeted and compelling. If your ICR is low, there may be issues with your targeting criteria, channel selection, placement strategy, or asset creative.

In the Lifetime Value Framework, this metric is used to calculate our cost per thousand impressions allowable.

See "Cost per Thousand Impressions"

See the "Lifetime Value Framework Allowables" cheat sheet

Impression Share–In pay per click advertising, the percentage of impressions your ads received relative to the total number of impressions in your market or category. For example, if insurance ads on TikTok received 1K total impressions this month, and your ads accounted for 500 of those impressions, then you would have a 50% impression share.

Impression share usually indicates how your pay per click spending and quality score compares to that of competitors: the more you spend and the greater the quality of your ads as ranked by the search engine, the greater your impression share. If your share drops while spending increases, then your ads likely need optimization.

Inbound Marketing–A marketing methodology that uses high-value content to attract and convert buyers. Inbound content often includes blogs, social media posts, webinars, and gated premium articles.

Inbound differs from other content-oriented marketing methods in that it specifically prioritizes organically earned attention over paid advertising. While this approach may generate fewer prospects, the prospects that it does yield tend to be more qualified. And these prospects appreciate the superior authenticity of inbound engagements relative to hard-sell engagements.

Note that the success of inbound marketing largely hinges on consistently achieving high search rankings for your target keyword set. This has become harder to achieve as the internet and online competition have grown.

See "Content Marketing"
See "Search Engine Optimization"

Incremental Lift–A metric expressing how much a particular marketing program/asset improves your target KPIs. Measuring incremental lift reveals the value of individual strategic shifts relative to your current performance, informing how you should proceed.

For example, you might measure how much conversions improve after adding a new channel to your marketing mix, or how much conversions decline when that channel is removed. The results will inform what channels you use going forward.

See "A/B Test" for another example of incremental lift testing.

Integrated Campaigns–Marketing campaigns that are strategically deployed across multiple channels and/or mediums, delivering a single, unified message. Some popular channels include social media, digital ads, email, direct mail, TV, radio, experiential, and out-of-home marketing.

Integration amplifies campaign reach, resonance, and memorability. It also generates more data points for honing personas and optimization.

See "Channel"
See the "Five-Tactic Marketing Framework" cheat sheet
See "Incremental Lift"

Internet of Things–The global network of internet-connected objects capable of collecting and sharing data. Examples of IoT devices include wearables, vehicles, appliances, manufacturing equipment, and smart thermostats.

As connected devices proliferate, marketers gain access to an expanding trove of customer data. This data powers precision targeting, campaign personalization, and other optimizations.

IoT–See "Internet of Things"

IVR–Acronym for interactive voice response. Refers to an automated telephone system that receives and routes calls, often used for customer service phone lines. Well-designed IVRs allow customers to self-serve instead of waiting on hold for an agent, and their interactive menus help triage calls efficiently, directing them to appropriate departments.

Unfortunately, poorly designed IVRs are much more common, and they can cause serious damage to your brand's customer experience.

See "Customer Experience"

Key Performance Indicators–Any metric used to gauge campaign performance. Some KPIs include revenue, leads generated, cost per lead, conversion rate, and customer lifetime value.

Once established, KPIs steer day-to-day decision-making. Dashboards help you track progress, and analytic reports help you turn KPI data into actionable insights.

Keywords–Specific words and phrases that prospects use online when searching for information related to your offerings. To ensure visibility and drive traffic, it's crucial that you integrate keywords into your digital assets. They should inform messaging, paid search bids, SEO optimization, and campaign targeting.

To identify keywords, analyze high-ranking sites, and conduct research and surveys with your audience. Also, assess search volume and competition. The most useful keywords will be the ones that are highly relevant, have high search volume, show high buying intent, and have low competition.

KPIs–See "Key Performance Indicators"

Last Click Attribution–An attribution model that assigns all credit for any given conversion to that customer's last interaction. This might include their final website visit, ad click, email open, or content download before adding to cart.

While simple to understand and calculate, last click attribution risks undervaluing or overlooking key interactions at the awareness and consideration stages. It can also incentivize excessive retargeting.

Ultimately, last click may misrepresent what actually caused your customer to buy.

See "Attribution"

Last Interaction Attribution—See "Last Click Attribution"

Leads—Prospects at the midpoint of your funnel, who have demonstrated interest or intent to buy by giving you some personal and/or contact information. Prospects can become leads by downloading content, requesting demos, or providing contact info. Generating and nurturing these leads is essential, setting the stage for eventual conversion.

See "Lead Conversion Rate"
See "Lead Generation"
See "Lead Scoring"

Lead Conversion Rate—A campaign efficiency metric, expressing how many leads it takes to generate one conversion. Lead conversion rate is calculated by dividing your total conversions by your total leads. Improving conversion rates grows revenue without necessarily increasing traffic or spending.

Raising your LCR makes your campaign more efficient, closing more deals without having to generate any additional prospects.

In the Lifetime Value Framework, this metric is used to calculate our cost per lead allowable.

See "Leads"
See "Cost per Lead"
See the "Lifetime Value Framework Allowables" cheat sheet

Lead Generation—The process of identifying, attracting, capturing, and nurturing prospects to become leads. Commonly abbreviated as "lead-gen." Some lead generation sources include ads, referrals, events, partnerships, demos, and gated content offers.

In lead generation, the goal is to collect prospect contact information and identify signals of their intention to buy. Marketing and sales departments then use this data to drive conversions.

See "Leads"

Lead Scoring–The process of ranking and prioritizing prospects. Lead scoring assigns points to individual leads based on characteristics like firmographics, job title, and channel of origin. These characteristics are then weighted by their correlation to historical conversion success.

Lead scoring enables businesses to pursue high-potential prospects before other prospects. It also informs messaging personalization.

At the most basic level, leads can be scored in two categories: hard and soft. Hard leads are those that have shown individual intent or initiative and are therefore qualified. Some examples would be leads collected from content marketing, demonstration signups, or any other initiative that requires the individual to enter their own information.

Soft leads are those that are not gathered in a way that requires qualification. Some examples of soft leads would be purchased lead lists, lists acquired in trade, or any other activity in which the individual did not provide the lead information themselves.

See "Leads"

See "Sales Qualified Leads"

Lifetime Value Framework–An advanced funnel tactic for resource allocation. The LVF helps you identify ideal spending targets ("allowables") for each stage of the funnel, rooting these targets in real-time performance data. This represents a departure from traditional marketing budgets, which often set arbitrary floors and ceilings, and/or rely on third-party investors to foot the marketing bill.

Deployed correctly, the Lifetime Value Framework prevents both underspending and overspending, insuring your campaign against losses and empowering you to scale aggressively.

See the "Lifetime Value Framework Allowables" cheat sheet
See the "Five-Tactic Marketing Framework" cheat sheet

Linear Attribution–An attribution model that gives equal credit to every channel touchpoint leading up to a conversion. It assumes that all interactions along the buyer's journey contribute equally to their final purchase.

While perhaps more accurate than some other attribution models, linear attribution can be unhelpful, making no actionable claims about where the highest-value interactions take place.

See "Attribution/Attribution Models"

Long-Tail Pattern–In statistics, a distribution pattern where values spike briefly, drop rapidly, then taper off slowly. In this book, we discuss the long-tail pattern in two contexts: customer lifetime value and campaign half-life.

In CLV, the long-tail pattern captures the uneven distribution of value across companies' customer bases, which often feature a few repeat heavy buyers and many occasional light buyers.

In campaign half-life, the distribution pattern recurs, illustrating that marketing campaigns tend to generate most of their deals early, then drop and taper off.

See "Campaign Half-Life"
See "Customer Lifetime Value"

Loyalty Programs–Incentive programs that reward recurring purchases. Perks for repeat buyers may include discounts, free gifts, early access to sales, and free shipping. These loyalty benefits often increase in parity with purchase volume or customer lifetime duration.

Loyalty programs can boost lifetime value by giving customers a reason to consolidate more of their category spending with one provider. But these programs can also backfire. The expense of such a program may not be worthwhile for every company, and any disruption of loyalty benefits can attract big brand backlash.

LVF–See "Lifetime Value Framework"

Machine Learning–A subset of artificial intelligence wherein software teaches itself to make decisions by studying large data sets. Theoretically, the more data fed into these self-learning models, the more accurate they become at executing tasks like predictive analytics, language processing, and graphic design.

For marketers, machine learning powers campaign ideation, automation, personalization, forecasting, attribution, optimized ad buys, asset generation, and much more.

See "Artificial Intelligence"

Market Research–The investigation of target customers and markets, aimed at informing campaign creative and operations. Some market research resources include surveys, focus groups, and existing published materials.

The goal is to identify granular details around consumer demographics, behaviors, attitudes, language, preferences, and unmet needs. These insights dictate brand positioning, guide campaign development, reveal new segments, and highlight growth opportunities.

When campaign strategists forego market research, they risk anchoring their campaigns to false assumptions—an expensive mistake.

Marketing Channel–See "Channel"

Marketing Mix–The combination of marketing channels used in your integrated campaign. The optimal mix for any campaign depends on budget, funnel stage, conversion objectives, competitive landscape, and audience.

Mixes should be refined over time based on performance data, customer response, and market testing.

See "Integrated Campaigns"

Marketing Personas–See "Customer Persona"

Marketing Qualified Leads–Prospects who match an ideal customer profile and exhibit key buying indicators. Because they match criteria for fit, readiness, and intent, MQLs are prime candidates for conversion. Once a lead is qualified by marketing, they are often passed on to sales for further qualification.

See "Ideal Customer Profile"
See "Sales Qualified Leads"
See "Lead Scoring"

MarTech–Software and platforms designed to support marketing teams. Some applications for MarTech include managing channels, performing analytics, and running automations.

Mental Availability–The likelihood of recalling and considering a particular brand while making a purchase decision. Ultimately, higher mental availability translates to a greater likelihood of customer acquisition.

Mental availability is built through repeated exposure to your brand and targeted messaging.

See "Mindshare"
See "Share of Voice"
See "Brand Marketing"

Micro-Yes–An affirmative response that's easy to give and has little-to-no stakes attached to it. Salespeople often warm up leads by asking low-pressure questions, each of which yields a micro-yes. The belief is that these small agreements create momentum toward conversion—the ultimate "yes."

Mindshare–The degree to which target audiences recall or consider your brand relative to alternatives. When evaluating mindshare, we imagine that every market category has a maximum quantity of attention. You and your competitors vie for this attention, each winning some share of it.

See "Mental Availability"

See "Share of Voice"
See "Brand Marketing"

MQLs–See "Marketing Qualified Leads"

Multi-Channel Campaigns/Marketing/Strategy–See "Integrated Campaigns"

Multi-Channel Performance Marketing–See "Multi-Channel Campaigns" and "Performance Marketing"

NDR–See "Net Dollar Retention"

Net Dollar Retention–A metric expressing revenue retention from existing customers, achieved via upsell, cross-sell, and renewals. Ideally, NDR should be 100% or higher.

To maintain 100% NDR, any drop-off in year-to-year recurring revenue will have to be replaced with new post-conversion sales. For this reason, high NDR is most easily achieved by maintaining low churn rates (i.e., curtailing customer attrition).

Neural Network–A method for building AI. Inspired by the design of the human brain, neural networks are composed of interconnected nodes, analogous to neurons. By altering the connections between nodes, neural networks identify patterns and relationships within data sets.

Neural networks represent the backbone of deep learning, which is a subtype of machine learning, which, in turn, is a subtype of AI. They show up in a variety of AI software services, including facial recognition, natural language processing, predictive modeling, and image generation.

See "Artificial Intelligence"
See "Machine Learning"

Nurture Campaign–Marketing campaigns designed to build trust among leads or prospects—often by providing educational content without a hard sell. Nurture campaigns prime prospects to make an eventual purchase, tailoring every message to that prospect's current location in the buyer's journey.

See "Content Marketing"

One-to-One Marketing–A marketing methodology characterized by hyper-targeted messaging. In one-to-one marketing, marketers tailor every message and product offered to the individual consumer, based on that consumer's particular wants and needs.

This approach is made possible by big data aggregation, AI analytics, and automated deployment tools. Benefits include boosted relevance, retention, and lifetime value.

OOBE–See "Out-of-Box Experience"

Organic Advertising–No-cost advertising where consumer attention is earned rather than bought. Some organic advertising efforts are within the marketer's sphere of influence: posting quality content on blogs and social, improving SEO, and designing strong email campaigns. Other organic assets are user generated, such as referrals and reviews.

See "Inbound Marketing"
See "Search Engine Optimization"

Outbound Marketing–A marketing methodology that pushes unsolicited messages out to potential prospects and customers. Some outbound practices include cold calling/emailing, direct mailing, tradeshow pitching, and door-to-door sales.

While outbound extends your reach further than inbound, response rates tend to be low. To overcome intrusiveness and deliver results, your outbound messaging must deliver genuine value to prospects.

Out-of-Box Experience–The customer's experience of unboxing, setting up, and making their first use of your product/service. Out-of-box design considerations may influence factors like packaging, onboarding, and initial functionality. These touchpoints create first impressions that carry lasting weight. Strong OOBE can establish affinity, familiarity, and positive brand associations that continue paying dividends long after conversion.

See "Customer Experience"

Paid Advertising–Any marketing assets that you pay to circulate. Common paid formats include social promotions, PPC ads, banner ads, sponsored content, TV commercials, radio spots, print ads, and out-of-home ads like billboards and transit posters. Paid ads amplify reach and impressions while delivering results more quickly than organic alternatives. Paid advertising can also complement organic and owned marketing efforts.

See "Organic Marketing"

Pay per Click–A digital marketing model in which you pay publishers whenever users click on your ads. PPC ads appear alongside organic search engine results and website content. Generally speaking, the more relevant and useful your ad, the higher your clickthrough rates will be.

One helpful PPC strategy is to focus on customers using keywords indicative of purchase intent. These might include phrases like "cheapest," "fastest," and "buy online."

See "Cost per Click"

Paywall–A monetization tool used by content publishers. Paywalls restrict the visibility of digital content, offering access only to those who pay or subscribe. They're commonly placed on high-value assets like whitepapers, webinars, premium articles, and research reports.

To overcome the friction inherent in paywalls, you must deliver content that is genuinely high value. Some publishers build trust first, using "soft" paywalls, which grant some access before requiring a purchase/subscription.

Performance Marketing–A marketing tactic designed to trigger direct, immediate action or response. Goals may include impressions, leads (downloads, phone calls, form submissions, etc.), and sales. Historically has also been called direct marketing or direct response marketing.

Performance marketers focus on generating measurable, attributable results through data-driven testing and optimization. Strategies usually incorporate transactional language, time-sensitive messaging, clickable UI, and aggressive tracking.

See the "Five-Tactic Marketing Framework" cheat sheet

Performance Metrics–Efficiency metrics that reflect actual current resources, spending, and results. (Contrast with projection metrics, which anticipate performance in hypothetical future scenarios.)

Performance metrics are crucial for directing real-time spending because they reveal how dollars spent today will perform. Comparing these metrics to goals and projections can also help inform long-term strategic planning.

See "Direct Method of Value Determination"

See "Projection Metrics"

Personalized Marketing/Personalization–See "One-to-One Marketing"

Personas–See "Customer Persona"

Position-Based Attribution–An attribution model that assigns credit based on each channel's place within the path-to-purchase. Specifically, position-based models give the largest share of credit (40% each) to first and last interactions, with the remaining 20% of credit spread evenly among all other interactions.

See "Attribution/Attribution Models"

See "First Click Attribution"

See "Last Click Attribution"

Post-Conversion–The funnel phase after leads convert into customers. Post-conversion extends from the initial purchase through the entire duration of the customer's relationship with your company. The goal of post-conversion marketing is retaining customers and maximizing their lifetime value via renewals, upsells, and cross-sells.

See "Renewal"

See "Upselling"

See "Cross-Selling"

See "Customer Lifetime Value"

See "Net Dollar Retention"

See "Remarketing"

PPC–See "Pay per Click"

Predictive Analytics–The use of data, machine learning, and statistical modeling to make predictions about future outcomes and behaviors. Predictive analytics supports planning and decision-making by forecasting future events like trends, buying patterns, and competitor action. This then guides marketing efforts, including segmentation, media buys, and message personalization.

Predictive Lead Scoring–See "Predictive Analytics"

Private Equity–A capital investment into a private company, usually made in exchange for majority ownership shares. In most cases, PE investors transition founders and other legacy stakeholders into limited partnerships while installing their own governance. The PE's objective is usually to "flip" the business: first they improve profitability and/or brand value, then they sell their shares for a profit.

Because PEs often value growth above all else, these investors may direct marketing teams to outspend their Lifetime Value Framework allowables.

Product–Market Fit–Conditions under which a product is likely to succeed. To achieve product–market fit, you must find a strong market and deliver a strong product. Namely, the market must be large enough and resource-rich enough to support profitability, and the product must satisfy a need in that market. The quality of fit improves if the potential for market monetization improves and/or product demand rises.

Programmatic Marketing–The automation of software to perform routine marketing functions like media buying, ad serving, personalization, and campaign analysis. Humans code the software, inputting goals and rules, then let the machines execute and scale.

Progressive Profiling–A sales technique wherein prospects complete a series of forms, each requesting more information than the last. Multiple touchpoints build trust while capturing increasingly useful data at each phase. Progressive profiling is typically deployed on gated, high-value content.

See "Gated Content"

Projection Metrics–Efficiency metrics that reflect hypothetical future resources, spending, and results (in contrast with performance metrics, which reflect actual current outcomes).

Projections allow you to make informed decisions about the future based on present data.

See "Performance Metrics"

Propensity Models–AI tools that score individuals on their probability of taking a specific action. These scores are generated through the analysis of web history, user characteristics, and first-party data. You can then use those scores to set individual, personalized allowables for every prospective customer.

See "Lead Scoring"

See "Predictive Analytics"

Prospects–Potential customers who demonstrate some early signal of

interest. Prospects fall between the awareness stage and the lead generation stage on the path to conversion. They are qualified targets who have
not yet been vetted or developed into leads.

Purchase Intent–Signals that a lead/prospect intends to make a
purchase in the short term. Quantifying intent can improve campaign
targeting, telling marketers which prospects should receive the most powerful conversion-oriented messages.

See "Lead Scoring"

Qualification/Qualified Leads–The process of gauging which leads
should be engaged by the sales teams. Qualified leads are the prospects
most likely to convert into customers. Qualification improves efficiency,
ensuring that the lion's share of conversion resources are spent on the
highest-probability prospects. Common evaluation criteria include readiness, budget, need, and authority.

See "Lead Scoring"

Remarketing–Targeting or re-engaging any previous prospects,
leads, or customers, sourced from any funnel stage and any channel—
digital or analog.

Remarketing pulls previous prospects back into the funnel. In the case of
pre-conversion targets, this can be more efficient than developing entirely
new prospects. In the case of existing customers, remarketing is crucial for
ensuring net dollar retention and boosting customer lifetime value.

See "Burn Pixel"
See "Net Dollar Retention"
See "Post-Conversion"
See "Retargeting"—a subtype of remarketing

Renewal–Extending an existing customer's subscription or contract.
Renewals are crucial for sustaining recurring revenue, which usually
costs less than acquiring new business. Ultimately, these renewals help

sustain and extend customer lifetime value, giving you more money to play with at every stage of the funnel. In this way, renewal is similar to the other two major post-conversion marketing efforts: upselling and cross-selling.

To pursue and improve renewal rates, you might improve customer experience, send automated renewal requests, or offer special incentives after expiration.

See "Post-Conversion"

See "Cross-Selling"

See "Upselling"

See "Customer Lifetime Value"

See "Net Dollar Retention"

Reporting Automations–Software that automatically delivers real-time campaign data and analytics, helping you break data silos, track performance, and respond to change rapidly. AI tools can greatly enhance reporting automations, studying larger data sets and delivering deeper insights.

Retargeting–A subtype of remarketing aimed at re-engaging prospects you previously saw or who interacted with your digital marketing assets, including websites, ads, and articles. When successful, retargeting combats attrition in the buyer's journey, increasing conversion rates.

See "Abandoned Cart Retargeting"

See "Burn Pixel"

See "Remarketing"

Retention–A company's ability to maintain customer relationships and continue earning revenue from each person post-conversion. High retention maximizes customer lifetime value and recurring revenue. To boost retention, companies might remarket to existing customers, improve customer support, build user communities, deliver valuable content post-conversion, and generally optimize the customer experience.

See "Net Dollar Retention"

See "Post-Conversion"

Return on Investment–A profitability metric expressing how much money was earned or lost on any given investment. In marketing, ROI is used to direct resource allocation and gauge whether campaigns meet their objectives.

To calculate ROI, divide net profit by total spend.

See "Key Performance Indicators"

Revenue–Income generated from business operations. In marketing, increased revenue usually indicates campaign success. Note however that some campaigns (like brand-based campaigns) may be successful without making a visible impact on revenue.

ROI–See "Return on Investment"

Sales Cycle–The time between a prospect's initial engagement and final conversion. B2B sales cycles are usually longer than B2C.

Note that long sales cycles usually extend the time it takes to see a marketing campaign's impact. If you evaluate these campaigns too early, you will get an inaccurate impression of performance.

Sales Plateau–Flat or declining sales performance that persists despite ongoing marketing investments. Escaping a plateau requires advanced marketing tactics.

See the "Five-Tactic Marketing Framework" cheat sheet

Sales Qualified Leads–Leads vetted, verified, and ranked by the sales team. Usually, these leads have been qualified by the marketing teams before being handed off to sales for further qualification. Because they match criteria for fit, readiness, and intent, SQLs are prime candidates for conversion.

See "Marketing Qualified Leads"
See "Lead Scoring"

Search Engine Optimization–Organic strategies for improving website visibility in search results pages. This visibility usually translates to free web traffic. Common SEO tactics include keyword integration and backlinking. Developing a robust library of blog content can further assist in SEO.

Note that SEO has become more difficult as the internet has grown—especially for small and emerging businesses.

See "Inbound Marketing"

Second-Party Data–Customer data exchanged, rented, or bought from another company. This is, in other words, another company's first-party data that has been shared with you or purchased by you. As a consequence, it's usually more robust, accurate, and useful than third-party data.

Common data partners might include complementary brands, trade organizations, or publishers. Common sources for purchase might include list brokerage services, database services, or data aggregation services.

See "First-Party Data"
See "Third-Party Data"

Segments / Segmentation–Grouping prospects according to common attributes that correlate to potential conversion and lifetime value. These might include factors like budget, industry, job title, web behavior, channel of choice, and campaign engagement history.

Sophisticated segmentation enables better targeting and deeper personalization. But beware: all segmentation must balance the benefits of personalization against its operational costs. There is such a thing as oversegmenting.

Sentiment Analysis–Evaluation of language to gauge attitudes toward brands, products, issues, etc. In marketing, sentiment analysis is most commonly applied to social media spaces, where AI tools can track emerging trends in real time.

Do posts about your brand trend toward the positive or the negative? The supportive or the critical? The delighted or the frustrated?

These insights can guide messaging strategy, customer experience design, and damage control campaigns.

SEO–See "Search Engine Optimization"

SERPs–Acronym for "search engine results pages," which are the listings produced in response to queries on Google, Bing, and other search engines. A higher SERP position usually translates to increased clicks and conversions.

See "Search Engine Optimization"

Share of Marke –A metric expressing the percentage of sales captured by a single brand in a given market category. SOM quantifies market penetration and dominance relative to competitors.

Growing your SOM usually requires expanding your marketing spend. When campaigns are executed well, this increased spending should win you extra share of voice, which should, in turn, deliver a larger share of market.

See "Extra Share of Voice"

Share of Voice–A metric expressing the percentage of messaging produced by a single brand in a given market category. SOV quantifies brand prominence and pervasiveness relative to competitors. Some SOV indicators include ad spends, media mentions, and impressions generated.

Boosting SOV improves brand awareness and mental availability, ultimately improving conversion rates. When your SOV exceeds your share of market, it can improve your company's sales position relative to competitors.

See "Extra Share of Voice"
See "Mental Availability"

Small and Midsize Business–A company whose employee and revenue numbers are lower, relative to enterprise corporations.

When competing with larger corporations, SMBs are underdogs, whose share of market and share of voice will suffer due to their limited budgets and power. Nevertheless, by strategically leveraging advanced marketing tactics, nimble flexibility, and niche advantages, these SMBs can still find paths to success.

SMB–See "Small and Midsize Business"

Social Media Listening Software–Tools that analyze social media conversations related to a brand or market category. Phenomena of interest may include brand mentions, post engagement, keyword trends, emerging sentiment, and centers of influence.

Marketers use listening to gauge campaign resonance, learn subcultural dialects, assess competitive standing, mitigate reputational threats, optimize personas, and uncover new opportunities.

See "Sentiment Analysis"

Social Proof–A psychological and sociological phenomenon in which individuals look to fellow community members as models for appropriate action. In marketing, social proof generally refers to testimonials, endorsements, reviews, bestseller lists, and other indicators of third-party validation. These and other forms of social proof can often do more to build brand trust than any ad or marketing asset.

SOM–See "Share of Market"

SOV–See "Share of Voice"

SQLs–See "Sales Qualified Leads"

System 1 Thinking & System 2 Thinking–A taxonomy of evaluative processes, introduced in Daniel Kahneman's *Thinking Fast and Slow*.

"System 1 thinking" refers to an evaluative process that is fast, intuitive, and emotional. Marketers play into this thinking system with brand marketing, which aims to establish positive emotional attitudes toward a company and/or its offerings.

System 2 thinking is slow, deliberate, and logical. This system is spoken to by content marketing, which aims to win business by educating prospects and establishing merit-based dominance.

Performance marketing is usually designed to put pressure on System 2, encouraging prospects to take immediate action despite limited information.

TAM–See "Total Addressable Market"

Third-Party Data–Consumer data collected by external brokers and sold to SMBs for marketing purposes. Data points may include contact info, demographics, purchase data, search history, and much more. Brokers are often major digital platform owners like Google and Meta.

Marketers use third-party data to support targeting and segmentation efforts. But third-party data can often be unspecific and/or inaccurate. As regulators continue cracking down on data collection, third-party data is likely to become less abundant and less useful.

See "First-Party Data"

See "Second-Party Data"

Time Decay Attribution–An attribution model that distributes credit among all channels, weighted based on their proximity to the final sale. The closer a channel was to the customer's conversion, the more credit that channel will receive.

This attribution model is particularly reliable for measuring channel performance on renewals and other deadline-motivated conversions. In other circumstances, time decay models risk undervaluing top-of-funnel engagements, which may be vital for generating interest and establishing trust. These oversights may be especially problematic in the case of long sales cycles, where prospects will likely move through many touchpoints before converting.

See "Attribution/Attribution Models"

Total Addressable Market–The total revenue opportunity available for a product when considering all possible buyers. Calculating TAM reveals headroom to scale up, suggesting the potential value of increasing marketing and sales spends.

Upselling–Selling product upgrades or augmentations to existing customers, post-conversion. These may include premium-tier products/services with features that increase capacity, speed, customizations, capabilities, warranties, support, or reduced time to customer (shipping and handling).

Upselling is one of the most powerful things you can do to drive up customer lifetime value, giving you more money to play with at every stage of the funnel. In this way, upselling is similar to the other two major post-conversion marketing efforts: cross-selling and promoting subscription renewals.

See "Renewal"

See "Post-Conversion"

See "Customer Lifetime Value"

VC–See "Venture Capital"

Venture Capital – Venture capital firms offer investment to startups and growth-stage companies in exchange for partial ownership. They profit by selling their shares during liquidity events.

Unlike private equities, VCs usually don't pursue majority ownership and don't install their own governance teams, although they often offer advice and mentorship to company leadership. VCs also tend to prefer young, high-risk/high-reward ventures, whereas private equities tend to prefer more established, more conservative ventures.

Because VCs often value growth above all else, these investors may direct marketing teams to outspend their Lifetime Value Framework allowables.

VOC–See "Voice of the Customer"

Voice of the Customer–Feedback collected directly from an organization's customer base through interviews, surveys, reviews, forums, etc. When made public, this feedback can have an outsized impact on brand trust.

See "Social Proof"

TOOLS AND RESOURCES

In the dynamic world of integrated marketing, tools and resources are constantly evolving. To stay ahead of the curve and ensure you're leveraging the latest advancements, it's crucial to have the newest tools at hand.

That's why I've created a dedicated section on my website where you can access a curated list of the most current and effective tools and resources by category.

Simply scan the QR code below to explore:

Link address: https://nickdoyle.com/resources

**FAST
COMPANY**
Press

CHEAT SHEET: FIVE-TACTIC MARKETING FRAMEWORK

The Five-Tactic Marketing Framework is my system for unifying some of the most powerful advanced marketing tactics available to SMBs. When deployed individually, each of these tactics is a powerhouse unto itself. But when leveraged together, the resulting framework is even greater than the sum of its parts, delivering results that initiate, boost, and secure long-term profitability.

The following are the five tactics:

1. **Brand and Performance Marketing:** promotion of your brand as a whole, concentrating on recognition and reputation; paired with promotion of your brand, products, or offerings, concentrating on profitable campaign performance vis-à-vis the Lifetime Value Framework.

2. **The Lifetime Value Framework:** an advanced funnel tactic that empowers marketers to reverse engineer spending allowables based on customer lifetime value.

3. **Understanding Your Customer:** the detailed research into understanding your target customer base(s) and their motivators.

4. **Integrated Campaigns:** the system by which we select, synchronize, and deploy messaging across marketing channels.

5. **Artificial Intelligence:** tools that can dramatically amplify the power of the preceding tactics, introducing new efficiencies and iterative possibilities.

You can read more about each of the five tactics in the Glossary.

CHEAT SHEET: LIFETIME VALUE FRAMEWORK ALLOWABLES

An advanced funnel tactic for resource allocation, the LVF helps you identify ideal spending targets ("allowables") for each stage of the funnel, rooting these targets in real-time performance data. This represents a departure from traditional marketing budgets, which often set arbitrary floors and ceilings, and/or rely on third-party investors to foot the marketing bill.

Deployed correctly, the Lifetime Value Framework prevents both underspending and overspending, insuring your campaign against losses and empowering you to scale aggressively.

The framework has the following five key metrics:

1. Customer Lifetime Value (CLV)

   The average revenue generated by a customer across their entire relationship with your company. Because it expresses how much revenue each customer will generate, CLV also becomes the basis for determining how much revenue we can spend to acquire those customers.

   **CLV = average duration that customer buys from company ×
   average order frequency per period × average order value**

2. Customer Acquisition Cost (CAC) Allowable

The amount we can afford to spend to acquire a new customer. For our purposes in this book, we will set this allowable equal to the average profit generated by a customer across their entire relationship with your company. This allowable determines how much you can spend in total across the entire funnel to acquire the next customer.

CAC allowable = CLV × average net margin

3. Cost per Thousand Impressions (CPM) Allowable

The portion of CAC that may be spent on generating impressions.

**CPM allowable = CAC allowable ×
average impression conversion rate**

4. Cost per Lead (CPL) Allowable

The portion of CAC that may be spent generating leads.

**CPL allowable = (CAC allowable − CPM allowable) ×
average lead conversion rate**

5. Cost per Acquisition (CPA) Allowable

The portion of CAC that may be spent converting leads into customers.

**CPA allowable = CAC allowable −
(CPL allowable + CPM allowable)**

For more on these metrics, see the Glossary.

INTRODUCTION

"I'm following best practices, but my sales are plateauing; I'm getting beat by the competition and I'm out of new marketing channels to try."

That's the distress call that I hear most often. SMB C-suiters max out their marketing budgets, then send up flares. Corporate directors signal for help when multi-channel investments don't deliver expected returns.

These marketers, sales specialists, and business leaders are doing everything right, but they're hitting a ceiling. They're tapping into all the mainstream channels, executing all the best practices, funneling like their lives depend on it, and yet they can't break past their plateaus or pull away from their competitors. They can't seem to increase sales. And their budgets are breaking.

There was a time when these conditions caused less concern. We considered them ordinary growing pains, and we rested easy in the knowledge that private equity and venture capital firms had the cure—more $$$. We could count on investors to swoop in and rescue us.

But today, we're living in a more grounded economic reality. For the most part, the blank checks have vanished. We must now operate within the bounds of our businesses' economics. On the rare occasions when investors do swoop in, they don't offer us any grace. They demand a clear path toward profitability, and they swoop right out again if we don't deliver.

Meanwhile, the global pandemic turned multi-channel marketing on its head. What once was nice-to-have has now become table stakes. Without a multi-channel digital presence, we're down before the cards are dealt. And that goes for all SMBs—traditional and e-com alike. When marketing channels get maxed out, it's no longer an academic problem. It's an existential threat.

All of this is further complicated by the proliferation of machine learning tools. The AI arms race is well underway, empowering competitors to generate more content, claim more channels, and win more mindshare. Without a strong show of force, sales plateaus threaten to become sales freefalls. Maxed-out channels threaten to become dead ones.

What's at stake of course is not just our businesses, but our careers and our futures, as well as the careers and futures of our direct reports. When marketing departments underdeliver, budgets get gashed. When the competition wins, heads roll. When our companies falter, we do too.

These are immense challenges. Serious stakes. But the way I see it, none of that pressure makes this work any less fascinating or any less fun. My father always said that the best work in the world was the work you'd do for free, and there's nowhere I'd rather be than in the cockpit of a struggling campaign—studying markets, running analytics, and developing solutions. There's no bigger thrill than pulling brands out of tailspins, punching the marketing throttle, and making sonic booms.

I've spent my career chasing these sales and marketing problems across brands, across contexts, and across the world. Enterprise and SMB. Traditional and e-com. Global. National. Regional. Local.

For me, the investigation began at IBM's Global Business Services in Hong Kong, where I handled web analytics and e-commerce for global brands like Ralph Lauren and Cathay Pacific. I studied Asian-Pacific cultures, the adaptation of existing brand identities to those cultures, and the implementation of new technologies region-wide.

Across the intervening years, I managed nearly two dozen of my own brands as the CEO of an SMB called Direct to Policyholder (DTPH). We acquired and revitalized legacy brands. We launched shiny new brands from nothing. And every time, we encountered, wrestled with, and prevailed over the problems of plateaued sales and maxed-out channels.

Along the way, I dissected technical and strategic applications of AI, machine learning, and other emerging technologies. I certified at Google and Maven. I graduated from Singularity University's executive program. I learned to pair business problems with technological solutions, implement those solutions, and troubleshoot tools when they fail. We used these innovative technologies to build pinpoint targeting, broad channel integration, rich performance analytics, and AI-powered campaigns.

Across all of that experience, the most powerful discovery has been this: that no single marketing strategy has all the answers. You can't break past a sales plateau with performance marketing alone. You can't out market the competition with only brand-based messaging. Multi-channel theory cannot single-handedly solve multi-channel problems. Funnel strategy requires other tools to power it. AI tools require deep frameworks and strategic applications in order to deliver.

That's why I've written this book—to share some of the advanced marketing tactics that combine to transform SMBs from underperformers into outperformers. When deployed individually, each of these tactics is a powerhouse unto itself. But when synthesized together, the resulting framework is even greater than the sum of its parts, delivering results that initiate, boost, and secure long-term profitability.

In brief, the central observation of this book is that the sales plateau problem already has a solution. The strategies and tools exist, in our textbooks and in the marketplace. These solutions may be advanced, they may be complex, but they are accessible to e-coms and traditional businesses alike. All that's needed is a system for unifying them—a system that I call the "Five-Tactic Marketing Framework."

These are the five key tactics that this framework synthesizes:

1. *Brand and Performance Marketing*—promotion of your brand as a whole, concentrating on recognition and reputation; paired with promotion of your brand, products, or offerings, concentrating on campaign performance vis-à-vis the Lifetime Value Framework.

2. *The Lifetime Value Framework*—an advanced funnel tactic that empowers marketers to reverse engineer spending allowables based on customer lifetime value.

3. *Understanding Your Customer*—the detailed research into understanding your target customer base(s) and their motivators.

4. *Integrated Campaigns*—the system by which we select, synchronize, and deploy messaging across marketing channels.

5. *Artificial Intelligence (AI)*—tools that can dramatically amplify the power of the preceding tactics, introducing new efficiencies and iterative possibilities.

If some or all of those already sound familiar to you, then you've come to the right place. This isn't a 101-course for learning best practices in multi-channel marketing or funnel design. This is an advanced, strategic guide for those who want to elevate their marketing to the 201 or 301 level. You won't learn what these strategies and tools *are*; instead, you'll learn how to implement them. How to put them in conversation. How to combine them in order to break past your sales plateau and resuscitate your multi-channel strategy.

To that end, this book is broken up into two parts. In Part I, we'll survey each of the tactics. Then in Part II, we'll combine them, illustrating what the Five-Tactic Marketing Framework looks like in practice.

Chapter 1 will start things off with an analysis of the first tactic—brand and performance marketing. Then Chapter 2 will introduce the second tactic of SMB marketing: the Lifetime Value Framework. We'll learn to reverse engineer a new kind of funnel-powered marketing budget using customer-value data. Chapter 3 will tackle an age-old topic and our third tactic, understanding your customer. Chapter 4 will explore the fourth tactic—integrated campaigns—teaching us to boost impact using deep insights about our targets. And each of these chapters will end with a survey of the fifth tactic: AI interventions, which, when applied, will exponentially expand our teams' capabilities, enhance our performance, and generate new strategic insights.

Then in Part II, we'll unify the five tactics, exploring how they interact at every level of the funnel. Chapter 5 will tackle acquisition, Chapter 6 will tackle conversion, and Chapter 7 will tackle retention/upselling. Finally, the book's Conclusion will pull all the threads together, distilling the Five-Tactic Marketing Framework down to its most fundamental components.

The age of "blank check" safety nets may be over. We may no longer be able to make do with a single successful channel. We may feel threatened by AI-powered competitors. But there is an upside to all that change: We now have no choice but to excel. We *must* prove profitability. We *must* prove reliability and consistency. We *must* become better marketers, better leaders, better sellers, better communicators, better strategists. In so doing, we will grow—as thinkers, as creators, as innovators. And our businesses will grow with us.

Let's stick the landing together.

—NICK DOYLE,
Ponte Vedra Beach, Florida
2025

PART I

The Five Advanced Marketing Tactics

In the introduction, I laid out my mission for this book—to introduce what I call the "Five-Tactic Marketing Framework," which combines brand and performance marketing, the Lifetime Value Framework, understanding your customer, integrated campaigns, and AI tools. Ultimately, this book will demonstrate the extraordinary power of deploying all five tactics in concert rather than in isolation. But before we can unify the five tactics, we need to understand each of them, individually.

To that end, this part of the book—Part I—will walk us through each of the five tactics, exploring how they work and what they entail. Occasionally, we'll consider some instances of unification, but our primary focus will be on studying each tactic in a vacuum. Then, in Part II, we'll bring the five tactics together, exploring how their combined power rolls out across the funnel, from impression through post-conversion.

Chapter 1 begins with brand and performance marketing—tactic #1.

CHAPTER 1

THE OPTIMAL BALANCE OF PERFORMANCE AND BRAND MARKETING

This is no lazy man's field.
—**CLAUDE HOPKINS**, *Scientific Advertising*[1]

Marketing gets more complicated every year. Traditionally, there were only a half dozen or so major marketing channels: print, TV, radio, direct mail, billboards, PR, and a few others. Now there are dozens, including websites, email, organic social media, social media ads, search advertising, online display ads, video, AR, VR, and many others. There are 10,000 marketing technology programs available.[2] And that number, in dozens of categories, grows every year.

But in another sense, marketing never changes. Marketing is still and always will be about understanding your customers and moving them to action. Underneath today's wild proliferation of tools and channels, marketing can still be broken down into these two major types.

Brand marketing is one half of the first tactic of our framework. It's designed to increase mental availability[3]—the likelihood that someone will think of you and your product when they are ready to buy. Ninety-five percent of B2B customers aren't interested in buying right now[4] but probably will be sometime in the future (tomorrow, next week, next month, in three years, five years, whenever). So, it's vitally important to build your mental availability among them.

Performance marketing is the second half of the first tactic in our framework. It's designed to get people to act now—to buy online, become a lead, download a piece of content, sign up for a webinar, visit a website, call an 800 number, etc. And, if it's required, to provide some contact information in return. Historically, it has also been called Direct Marketing or Direct Response Marketing.

Of course, both of these tactics are well-established, and there's an endless database out there of great 101-level content for both brand and performance marketing. But here's the trouble: the two are usually studied in isolation. One marketer becomes passionate about branding and devotes themselves to it. Another becomes passionate about performance and becomes likewise devoted. But both are missing something vital. They're missing the extraordinary power of the two tactics combined.

Throughout this book, we'll see, again and again, how the highest-performing businesses unlock extraordinary opportunities when they unite all five tactics of SMB marketing. And that begins here—with the unification of brand and performance marketing.

Sometimes companies combine both brand and performance messages into the same "brand response" ads, such as GEICO's creative TV commercials with their ubiquitous "Fifteen minutes could save you 15% or more" tagline. These brand response ads can be effective, although both the brand and performance effects are usually weaker than with purely brand or performance campaigns.

It's not a matter of either/or. You need both brand and performance marketing, in part because strong brand and brand marketing programs will make your performance marketing more effective.

And I'm going to give away the ending right now and say that you should split your B2B marketing efforts roughly 50/50 between brand and performance.[5] One is not "better" than the other; most companies will grow the fastest by using both, often in thoughtful combinations.

— *SIDEBAR* —

THE NEW LAWS OF MARKETING

These days, marketers (and the executives we report to) commonly say that "we should be driven by data." Usually, by this, people mean that we should be driven by *our* data—the data from our company and campaigns. That data is often small, though, and sometimes not even statistically significant.

But because of the results of the published research of others, based on thousands of cases in hundreds of industries, we now have laws of marketing that simply weren't known before. We should be driven by that data, too, and take advantage of these insights, which are central to this chapter.

Some of these sources include:

- Byron Sharp, director of the Ehrenberg-Bass Institute for Marketing Science in Australia. His book, *How Brands Grow*, based on Ehrenberg-Bass's decades of experience with major brands, is one of the most important recent contributions to marketing.

- Les Binet, group head of effectiveness at adam&eveDDB in London, and Peter Field, marketing consultant, have put out several reports based on The Institute of Practitioners in Advertising (IPA) database of 1,000 award-winning campaigns. The IPA awards are based on results, not subjective critiques of design or creative.

- Mark Ritson, marketing professor and consultant to major brands, did an analysis of the Effie's database, which comprises over 5,000 award-winning campaigns in the United States and overseas.[6] Effie awards are also based on documented results.

continued

- Paul Dyson, founder of Data2Decisions, a UK agency that has won many IPA and Effie awards, put out a study of lessons learned from their 1,500+ campaigns.[7]

- Jenni Romaniuk, research professor at Ehrenberg-Bass, co-authored *How Brands Grow, Part 2* with Byron Sharp and wrote the influential *Building Distinctive Brand Assets*.[8]

- The B2B Institute[9] is a think tank funded by LinkedIn that researches the future of B2B marketing and decision-making. It has commissioned studies from Binet and Field as well as others.

- Robert Johnson, vice president and principal analyst at IDG Connect, did research with Kim Wallace of Wallace & Washburn that involved surveying tens of thousands of B2B tech buyers in the United States.

- And many others, some of whom you'll find in the endnotes of this book.

We don't expect every new physicist to rediscover Newton's Laws or Einstein's theories—of course, they should stand on the shoulders of others—and so should we in marketing.

THE VALUE OF A STRONG BRAND

Every year since 1998, market research firm Kantar has released its BrandZ Top 100 Most Valuable Global Brands report. (This is an example of content marketing to build a brand, something that we'll be discussing a lot.) At the time of writing, Apple, Amazon, Google, and Microsoft have shared the top four slots for five straight years, with brands valued between $200 billion and $947 billion.[10]

Many researchers have documented the value of a strong brand. They include aspects such as the following:

- More people know the company and their offerings.

- The company achieves more impact from their marketing.[11]

- They are more likely to be remembered when someone wants to buy something that they sell (mental availability).

- The company has more customers *and* customers who each buy slightly more than the fewer customers of small companies (what Andrew Ehrenberg first described in 1969 as the marketing Law of Double Jeopardy).

- Customers are less price sensitive, so the brand can achieve higher margins.

- Customers are less likely to leave after one bad experience.

- And so on.

For example, in a store, the branded product often sells for 20–30% more than the generic one—even when, in the case of generic pharmaceuticals, they are chemically identical.

Amazon is about three decades old, with a brand value in the hundreds of billions. What is the value of your company's brand? What could it be in 30 years?

Martin Kihn of Gartner writes, "The point of brand messages, including advertising, is to build brand value, which is directly related to profits. A brand's value is the premium consumers are willing to pay over a generic version of the same thing. Investing in brand advertising is a way to avoid competing only on price."[12]

While performance marketing can produce a rapid sales uplift, brand marketing reduces price sensitivity and improves margins, thereby generating higher profits.

Building a brand is based on building strong memories, and that is generally done through emotional messages and experiences, not logical arguments and persuasion.

Byron Sharp puts it this way: "Neuroscience and psychology have recently advanced our understanding of how memories and brains work. These discoveries have important implications for advertising, because advertising works by creating and refreshing memories. It is now known that much thinking and decision-making is non-conscious and emotional. Yet traditional theories of advertising are based on a dated view that we are usually rational (occasionally emotional) decision-makers, with near perfect memories."[13] You can replace "advertising" in that quote with "brand marketing" because all forms of brand marketing work the same.

The people making decisions for a business are actually the same human beings who make decisions for consumer purchases. And we decide with emotion and justify with logic most of the time.

Based on surveys of over 50,000 B2B tech customers, Robert Johnson at IDG Connect wrote, "B2B buyers react to emotional 'triggers' in many ways just like consumers do, but don't try to tell buyers that because they'll claim they err on the side of rational thought, because that's what they believe they are paid to do."[14]

Scott Magids, Alan Zorfas, and Daniel Leemon agree in *The Harvard Business Review*, "Our research across hundreds of brands in dozens of categories shows that it's possible to rigorously measure and strategically target the feelings that drive customers' behavior. We call them 'emotional motivators.' They provide a better gauge of customers' future value to a firm than any other metric, including brand awareness and customer satisfaction, and can be an important new source of growth and profitability."[15]

Performance messages tend to be very logical and demand a decision now: get 20% off, sign up for this webinar, download this report, schedule an appointment with a sales rep, etc.

But brand messages weigh the emotional component far more heavily, as this graph from Binet and Field illustrates.

Messages vs Emotions in B2B

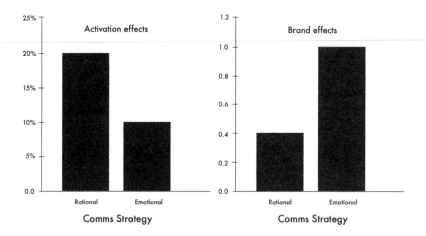

Over time, these emotional messages accumulate and prime the mind to remember and be positively disposed toward the brand. The following chart, also from Binet and Field, illustrates this.

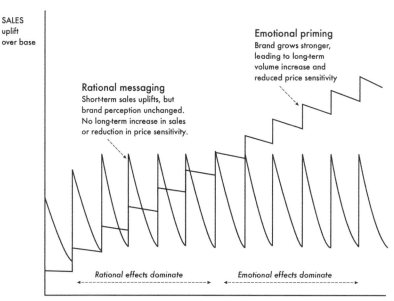

The jaggies across the bottom illustrate performance campaigns ("activation" in the UK terminology of Binet and Field). They can have a quick immediate effect, but their impact also degrades quickly.

The diagonal staircase represents brand marketing. Each encounter produces a smaller effect, but because of its strong emotional component, these degrade far less quickly. Instead, they accumulate over time. And after two to three years (the time it takes for brand campaigns to hit peak effectiveness), they produce a greater business impact than the performance campaigns.

No one remembers ads like these for email marketing software five minutes later. You either act on them immediately, or their effect is gone.

The brand staircase illustration isn't quite accurate, though. As the strength of the brand grows, it makes the performance campaigns more successful, too. On the right, after the brand staircase rises above them, the performance campaigns should be trending up slightly. So, a strong brand helps performance because of the emotional priming. (Are you more likely to respond to a campaign from a company that you know and trust or from one that you have never heard of?) But many performance campaigns do not add up to build a strong brand.

The performance ads are more *efficient* in the short run, but the brand marketing has greater long-term *effectiveness*.

One traditional model of marketing is "The 4 Ps":[16]

- Product

- Price

- Place

- Promotion

While people commonly think of marketing as just promotion, in fact, all four of these fall under marketing's umbrella and can have a profound impact on the long-term growth of a brand. Leonard M. Lodish and Carl F. Mela gave this example in *The Harvard Business Review*:

> An example of a company that has considered the effects of distribution ["Place" in the 4 Ps] is Lacoste, known for tennis shirts adorned with a tiny alligator. When the French company started selling the shirts in the United States in the 1950s, they became a fashion rage. General Mills acquired the brand in 1969, and it continued to sell well. However, in the mid-1980s, General Mills lowered the price on the shirts and broadened distribution to include discount outlets instead of adding high-end stores. The short-term effect was predictable: Sales increased. Yet the brand went from elite stores' racks to clearance bins and lost its cachet. Lacoste repurchased the brand in 1992. The company limited distribution to higher-quality clothing retailers, advertised the brand through celebrities, and raised prices. A change in

senior leadership in 2002 precipitated an even stronger brand focus. Since that time, sales have jumped 800%. However, in the initial years after Lacoste repurchased the brand, the company's marketing efforts had little immediate effect on revenues. Had the company assumed a short-term sales perspective, it may not have been able to reinvigorate the brand.[17]

Adidas: We over-invested in digital advertising

Adidas admits that a focus on efficiency rather than effectiveness led it to over-focus on ROI and over-invest in performance and digital at the expense of brand building.

About 10 years ago, Adidas made the mistake of turning away from brand marketing by focusing too much on short-term results, leaving the brand marketing to Nike. This was a classic case of single-tactic thinking. After just a few years, Adidas realized its mistake and reversed course, as this headline from 2019 explains.[18]

It's important to note that, as AI grows more powerful and more accessible, brand marketing is only going to become more important. AI proliferation makes it easier to start new businesses and launch new campaigns. That means more competitors and more noise in the marketplace. To differentiate ourselves, make ourselves heard, and lock down mindshare, we'll need to put serious blood, sweat, and dollars into our brands.

Building consumer trust will be particularly important, assuring customers that our businesses aren't merely automated scams. This means building customer relationships over time, beginning with the first interaction and continuing through the lifetime of the product and/or service.

This trust must be at the forefront of all brand-building efforts. Without it, there will not be true brand-based value.

— *SIDEBAR* —

SYSTEMS 1 & 2

Daniel Kahneman won the 2002 Nobel Prize in Economic Sciences, although he is primarily known as a psychologist. (This Nobel Prize may have been shared with his collaborator of many years, Amos Tversky, had he not died in 1996; Nobel Prizes are not awarded posthumously.) Kahneman and Tversky did decades of pathbreaking research into how our brains make decisions. For example, they first introduced the idea of "anchoring" in 1974. Anchoring is when decisions are affected by a reference point or "anchor." Retailers use anchoring all the time by establishing a high "normal" price and then putting the item on sale since people are more inclined to pay a price that they think is a bargain. Mark it up to mark it down.

In his 2011 book, *Thinking Fast and Slow*, Kahneman introduces the idea of Systems 1 & 2. System 1 is fast, instinctive, and emotional. System 2 is slower, deliberative, and logical.[19]

When we are building up brand associations in the minds of customers, we're encouraging their System 1 thinking. While they may not be interested in buying our offering right now, we want it to be top of mind when they are ready. And at that critical moment, they will tend to rely on what's known and comfortable rather than make the effort to find more alternatives.

Familiarity does not breed contempt; it breeds comfort and acceptance. A brand that we see over and over is more likely to come to mind in a positive way when we are ready to buy. Kahneman describes how we would need significant contrary information for System 2 to override System 1.

He writes, "A general 'law of least effort' applies to cognitive as well as physical exertion. The law asserts that if there are several ways of achieving the same goal, people will eventually gravitate

continued

to the least demanding course of action. In the economy of action, effort is a cost, and the acquisition of skill is driven by the balance of benefits and costs. Laziness is built deep into our nature."[20]

We are not as consciously aware of our System 1 thinking, but it dominates how we make decisions.

Performance marketing is usually designed to put pressure on System 2, encouraging prospects to take immediate action despite limited information.

HOW TO BUILD A BRAND

As some of the previous examples illustrate, any and all of the 4 Ps can contribute to building your brand. If we just focus on promotion for now, though, you need to achieve "extra share of voice" (ESOV).

This chart from Binet and Field illustrates the relationship between share of voice (SOV) and share of market (SOM). When a company's

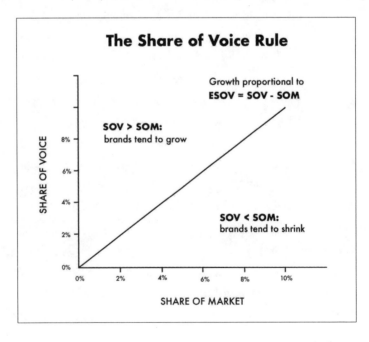

The Share of Voice Rule

Growth proportional to
ESOV = SOV - SOM

SOV > SOM:
brands tend to grow

SOV < SOM:
brands tend to shrink

SHARE OF VOICE

SHARE OF MARKET

SOV is about the same as its SOM, it tends to not be outgrowing its competitors. Companies with SOV above their market share (above the line) tend to grow, and those with SOV below the line tend to shrink.

To grow, be loud.

Venture capitalists (VCs) know this. Software companies typically spend about 15% of their budgets on marketing. But venture-backed startups spend 30–40% of their budgets on marketing so they can achieve considerable ESOV. VCs are investing in rapid growth, and they know that marketing is the way to produce it.

And while size is the biggest multiplier of marketing, creative is the second biggest. While small companies can't do much about the former, they definitely can compete with better creative.[21]

Any kind of promotional marketing can contribute to a company's SOV:

- Advertising

- Podcasts

- Webinars

- Blogs

- White papers

- Thought leadership pieces

- Infographics

- Emails

- Events

- Social media

- PR ("free media")

Your brand content will need to appeal to the different emotions of customers in different stages of their buyer's journey. In the top-of-funnel awareness stage, you'll be building trust through quality content about a range of industry topics. In the consideration stage, you can start to appeal to the specific buying criteria of different customer personas (see Chapter 3). Since B2B customers rarely trust (logical) ROI claims and put a higher premium on such factors as reliability, ease-of-use, and their personal professional success, in this phase you may be more successful with emotional appeals like social proof and phrases like on-time, hassle-free, and guaranteed.[22] As it used to be said, "No one gets fired for hiring IBM."

As we've said before, the key here is *building trust*. One of the most powerful ways to do that is by making a customer promise, then delivering on it. That follow-through is key to building trust in personal relationships, and business relationships are no different. In a piece for *The Harvard Business Review*, Roger L. Martin, Jann Schwartz, and Mimi Turner discussed the power of these promises:

> Consider these three promises from competitors in the same industry: Allstate's "You're in good hands," "Nationwide is on your side," and Geico's "15 minutes could save you 15%." Only Geico's is direct and verifiable. It promises that just 15 minutes of your time can save you 15% over your current insurance. That creates a connection. And if you take the 15 minutes and save 15% (or more), the company has built trust. Allstate and Nationwide imply promises— but essentially about themselves rather than the customer: Our hands are good hands, and we are on your side. Their promises aren't verifiable. What does "good" mean in practice? And how does "on your side" play out?
>
> Those differences made us wonder: Could the success of a brand-building campaign be related to the type of promise it made?[23]

Their answer was an unequivocal yes. Customer promise campaigns outperformed others by large margins on some of the most important brand-building metrics. The strongest promises they discovered were emotional benefit (Mastercard's "priceless" promise), functional benefit (FedEx's overnight promise), and ease of use (Uber's "smartest way to get around"). When building a brand campaign, they recommended using this litmus test:

> . . . Ask four simple questions: (1) Is the campaign based on a clear and unambiguous customer promise? (2) Were customer insights used to identify a promise that customers value? (3) Is the promise framed in a way that is truly memorable? (4) Were product, marketing, sales, and customer experience involved to ensure that it will be consistently fulfilled?[24]

Of course, making the right promise is one thing. Choosing the right channels and methods is quite another. For instance, video/TV ads are especially impactful when it comes to conveying emotions and building a brand. Stories and characters are especially useful in TV commercials. Video ads can be effective online.

HubSpot is a marketing software company that was founded in 2006. It developed and evangelized the "inbound marketing" approach built on many content offerings. It was putting out several pieces of content in all formats—*every day*. It certainly spent tens of millions of dollars on it, and possibly hundreds of millions. That large content library continues to generate tremendous value. SEO tool SpyFu estimates that every month HubSpot gets 6.7 million clicks on search and that it would have to pay over $14 million per month to achieve those results with paid ads.[25] Less than 20 years after its founding, HubSpot is a public company with over 143,000 customers and a market cap of $16 billion.

A new company offering marketing software would probably not be able to achieve the same results today with a similar investment in inbound marketing, though. If you're in a new industry or one in which your competitors are not putting out much content, you may be able to move the needle rapidly by producing, distributing, and amplifying content. If you're in an industry like MarTech in which countless pieces of content have been created over the past 20 years by thousands of companies, it will be considerably more difficult.

A company that wants to build its brand should work toward achieving salience among its potential customers. Fifteen years ago, HubSpot could do that mainly through content. What would work for your company?

Using Performance Marketing to Generate Rapid Results

For optimal growth, you need to combine all five tactics of the Five-Tactic Marketing Framework. That includes a combination of brand and performance marketing.

As we discuss in detail in later chapters, the most important elements for performance campaign success are the following:

- Audience—if you're not targeting the right people, nothing else you do matters.

- Offers—compelling offers can have a several hundred percent impact on campaign results.

- Creative—the copy, images, colors, landing page layouts, etc.

And, contrary to the jaggies/staircase chart we've seen, performance campaigns are not always quick affairs; they may be ongoing for some time, with constant optimization.

In this chapter, we've cited *Harvard Business Review* articles a few times. *HBR*, of course, is a business itself, and it has to constantly attract and retain new customers. It has one of the strongest brands in the business world. Nonetheless, it uses performance marketing to close the deal with new subscribers.

HBR's Marketing Director Jeff Levy noted in 2017 that response from their physical direct mail campaigns was declining, and its cost per acquisition (CPA) was high. So, *HBR* moved to a digital-first approach. "Using digital channels such as paid social, search and content marketing helped deliver a lower CPA, faster feedback on campaign performance, and highly scalable campaigns," said Levy.[26]

HBR uses its world-class content to engage potential subscribers. For example, it offered access to its archive of "Big Ideas" stories for 30 days, which then went behind a paywall. Visitor engagement with content is a strong indicator of interest and triggers subscription offers delivered via email and remarketing. Abandoned shopping cart retargeting was *HBR*'s lowest CPA.

Through this performance marketing program, *HBR* transformed its customer acquisition efforts. They reduced their total spend by 15% while producing an 11.8% increase in paid circulation to *HBR*'s highest level ever—over 308,000 subscribers.[27]

MEASURING THE GROWTH OF YOUR BRAND

How will you know that your brand-building efforts are working during the first two to three years that it takes for them to reach peak effectiveness?

Companies have many ways in which they can measure the value of their brand, including customer panels, surveys, price elasticity, churn, and the sales lift that they get from price discounts (the bigger the lift, the weaker the brand). Sales discounts have the very real possibility of hurting your brand in the long run, and they should be used with extreme caution.

Some of these techniques may be too expensive for SMBs or, like price discounts, may not apply to many B2B companies. Here are ways that you can identify growing brand strength.

For most companies, the most common search term bringing people to their site is their name, so organic search-generated traffic can be a good indicator of success. Steady, consistent growth in user count can be a good indicator that your organic search strategy is beginning to pay off.

Growth in links from other sites to yours is a good indicator, too, as is a steadily increasing number of mentions in the media.

In some industries, social mentions and strong sentiment analysis are good signs, and many tools can provide this data. Here is an example dashboard from one of the many data visualization tools on the market.

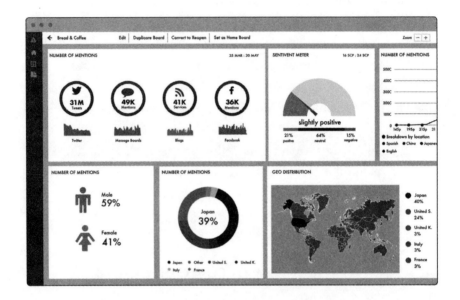

Google Trends, which shows relative search volume for particular terms, can be a good measure of market share. In the following chart, you see how HubSpot (top line) outstripped two competitors starting around 2009.

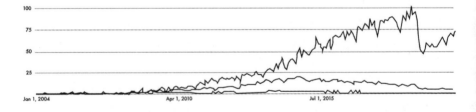

But HubSpot, with $1.3 billion in revenue in 2021, is pretty small compared to Salesforce with $24.6 billion in revenue in 2021.[28]

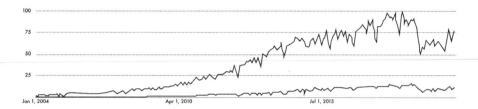

The impact seen in the data around 2020 can be attributed to the rapid change in market conditions with the onset of the COVID pandemic.

HOW TO GET STARTED

If you already have a robust marketing program, adopting the framework that I've described in this chapter will be fairly straightforward. You may need to optimize your performance program with the methods that I describe in the rest of this book. And you may need to elevate your brand marketing spend over two or three years until you achieve the optimal 50/50 balance. Along the way, you can use the brand metrics to track your progress.

But what if you don't have much of a marketing program going? What if you're not currently spending the 10–12% of your budget on marketing that mature B2B companies do?[29] (It's higher in some industries, like software, and lower in others like manufacturing and energy.) How do you start? Are you really going to go to the CEO and propose a strategy in which half of the budget won't have its maximum impact for two or three years? How likely is that to be approved?

One of the concepts that we discuss in this book is how you must start with the most effective channels and mediums first—those that will have the greatest return the fastest. Once you've grown sales and built credibility, and as those channels and mediums reach diminishing returns regarding investment, you should move to the next most efficient channel or medium. Broadly, this will mean starting with performance marketing and moving on to more brand-centric marketing, which will be more effective in the long run. Louis Gudema explains this approach in his *Bullseye Marketing* book.[30]

First, take advantage of your existing marketing assets. You have these, and it would be quick and inexpensive (often free) to put them to use.

- Improve your website messaging so it's not just about your offerings but also speaks to the pains and concerns of your customers.

- Add calls to action and landing pages throughout your site and other marketing and optimize them.

- Use your email list much more frequently. It's almost free to send emails, and they're highly cost-effective. Build to a once-a-week cadence; ultimately, you may even send them more frequently.

- Sell more to current customers; it's low-hanging fruit.

- Improve the collaboration between your sales and marketing teams, and implement a targeted account program.

In phase two, get in front of companies that plan to buy soon by using search advertising and first- and third-party intent data.

When you've achieved results (sales) and built credibility with these programs, you can go on to growing your brand marketing, which is phase three.

In this chapter, I've talked about two kinds of marketing: brand and performance. But there's a third kind, and it is probably the most common: bad marketing.

Bad marketing doesn't have any strong emotional or creative messages and so it doesn't build a company's mental availability, and it isn't performance marketing, so it doesn't produce any immediate leads or sales. It's a waste of money. It is primarily focused on the company's products and describes features in a way that interests very few who see it. Don't do it.

BRAND AND PERFORMANCE
MARKETING ENABLED BY AI

In the Introduction, I said that we'd be covering five tactics of SMB marketing: brand and performance marketing, the Lifetime Value Framework, understanding your customer, integrated campaigns, and AI tools. In this section—Part I—we're exploring those tactics independently. Then in Part II, I'll demonstrate how you can bring all five tactics to bear on each stage of the marketing funnel.

So far, in this chapter, we've taken our initial deep dive into the first tactic: brand and performance marketing. The next chapter will look at the Lifetime Value Framework. And the two chapters after that will address integrated campaigns.

Meanwhile, AI's going to be handled a bit differently.

From here on out, after every chapter, we will examine tactic #5—artificial intelligence—and discuss how it intersects with that chapter's topic. We won't cover specific, branded tools or apps as selecting precisely the right tool for your company is a delicate matter, not well-served by one-size-fits-all recommendations (however, there is a list of tools by category available on my website for free). Instead, we'll discuss the most powerful use cases for AI, discovering how these technologies create new possibilities and efficiencies for SMB marketing departments.

At the time of writing, the marketing community is abuzz with AI chatter—celebrations, condemnations, and prognostications of all kinds. On one side are those who say that this is the dawn of a new era in technology. On the other are those who speculate that AI is a passing fad, unworthy of our attention. I would suggest that both sides are wrong.

AI is, in fact, very old news. It's here to stay. And, frankly, it doesn't matter much whether it improves, or at what rate. If there's never another advancement in the field, marketing will still have been changed forever.

Alan Turing fired the starting gun in 1950, when he set computer science in motion and raised philosophical questions about machine sentience. Six years later, Dartmouth College hosted a summer research project on what it dubbed "artificial intelligence." And by 1959, Arthur Samuels was introducing "machine learning" as a promising new means for achieving functional AI. Four decades later, IBM's "Deep Blue" super-computer challenged world champion Gary Kasparov to a game of chess and won. And AI has only improved since then.

My point: the apparently sudden AI boom of the 2020s isn't just hype. It isn't a fad. It's the culmination of seven decades' worth of painstaking research and innovation. We certainly are experiencing a dramatic uptick in visibility and accessibility, but the most important vectors of change haven't been superficial—they've been material. AI isn't booming because Watson hired himself a publicist. It's booming because technologists finally have access to the resources that serious AI requires: hardware, data, and dollars.

First came the hardware. In 1965, the engineer Gordon Moore pre-dicted that the number of transistors on an integrated circuit would double every year. As it turns out, he was basically right. Now, after 60 years of exponential improvement, our GPUs and TPUs finally have the computational power necessary to run AI programs at scale.

After hardware came the data. AIs are very elaborate, very powerful probability-calculating machines. They simulate intelligence by predict-ing what word will come next in a sentence, what move will come next in a chess match, and what shape a cellular protein will take after it's translated from a sequence of mRNA. To make these predictions, AIs require huge, monstrous data sets. The huger and more monstrous, the better. These data sets then need to be segmented and labeled so that the software can make sense of them.

Generating, segmenting, and labeling enough data to win a chess match is a tall order, to be sure. But generating, segmenting, and label-ing enough data to write like a human or predict consumer behavior is another matter entirely. It's only with the advent and growth of the inter-net (as well as the internet of things) that sufficiently large data sets have become available.

Lastly come the dollars. Now that the first two resources are finally available at scale, Big Tech is ready to invest. Ditto investment groups and individuals. And where money goes, innovation follows.

The upshot for SMB marketers is that AI is here to stay. Businesses that don't adapt and adopt will not survive. In particular, the coming chapters will illustrate the importance of deploying AI across three major areas: Creation, Operation, and Optimization.

Creation

This book is all about making marketing more scientific, more rational, and more predictable. But there's no denying that our discipline is, at its core, a creative one. It takes creative leaps of empathy to understand our customers, just as it takes creative leaps of ingenuity to conceptualize campaigns. From there, other creative disciplines take over—copywriting, art, video, and experiential.

Generative AI has the power to expand both the volume of that creative work and its efficiency. It can develop customer personas, perform campaign ideation, and create campaign materials. AI can summarize research and help us connect the dots. It can propose elaborate channel-specific plans. It can write tweets, blogs, and keyword lists. And it can do these things in the blink of an eye.

Admittedly, generative AI often performs imperfectly, misrepresenting facts or offering sub-optimal solutions. But new tools don't need to be perfect to transform our industry. By generating first and second drafts in an instant, AI has the power to jumpstart creative work, completing the first phase of ideation at virtually no cost and in virtually no time at all. It may not get us all the way to final drafts, but it does have the power to shorten our timelines by hours, days, and even weeks.

This is why I say that it doesn't matter whether the tech improves or at what rate. In its current form, generative AI is already positioned to incite radical change. And generative AI is just the tip of the iceberg.

Operation

Next, we have *operation*: running campaigns, monitoring results, and recommending real-time changes. This is where narrow, task-specific, data-oriented tools come into play.

Take attribution for instance. Quantifying the discrete impact of individual channels is perhaps one of the most difficult, complex tasks in performance marketing. But it's not particularly difficult or complex for AIs. These tools can rapidly consider multiple attribution models and recommend the most pertinent ones. They can also improve the data that feeds our attribution models, helping us track engagements across browsers, devices, and usernames.

AI can likewise study other kinds of data sets to identify patterns and trends, tackling massive matrices that are far beyond human capacity. It used to take large teams huge swaths of time to compare lead sets with prospective sets with current customer sets and generate cross-segment insights. With AI, that work becomes no trouble at all. And once the numbers have been crunched, we no longer need humans to design data visualizations either. AI can do that too.

Optimization

All of these same capabilities can then be put toward our third major area of effect: *optimization*. AI can help us identify sales trends, track profitability by product line, and calculate the best possible application of general administrative expenses. For marketing departments in particular, AI modeling and analysis can deepen our understanding of how campaigns perform today and how prospective campaigns might perform in the future.

These creation, operation, and optimization implementations are quickly becoming ubiquitous. Businesses that don't tool up will not survive competition with AI-powered incumbents and disruptors. That's why we'll be returning to this topic at the end of every chapter, offering new insights. The goal is to capture as many use cases as we can across all three domains.

That work begins here: you'll find five use cases for AI as it pertains to brand and performance marketing. In the chapters that follow, we'll similarly survey possible use cases around the Lifetime Value Framework and integrated campaigns. Then, in Part II, we'll use the same approach to explore AI's utility at each stage of the funnel.

By the end of our time together, it should be clear that AI is not an isolated consideration. Like the first four tactics of SMB marketing, it must be deployed in conversation with other frameworks and strategies. Ultimately, a modern marketing team must draw on all five tactics in order to break past sales plateaus, dial up its KPIs, and realize its full potential.

AI USE CASES:
BRAND AND PERFORMANCE MARKETING

Creation
Campaign Ideation

Bring generative AI into your ideation process, using it to help set the direction for brand and performance campaigns. AI can "brainstorm" new campaign ideas based on specified criteria such as target market, seasonality, past performance, price point, etc.

Campaign Material Creation

Once you've set the direction, generative AI can also help you create campaign materials, including imagery, text, and video.

Marketing Mix Modeling

AI can help you select channels and allocate resources across them. First, plug in all the context for your campaign: personas, historical sales data, product type, etc. Then the AI will model various campaigns and help you choose the best option.

Operation
Market Message Testing

First, use these tools to understand what tests will have the biggest impact and where. Then run those tests across multiple channels, searching for optimal results.

Optimization
Ad Spend Forecasting and/or Projection

AI can study historic campaign metrics and use them to forecast changes to customer lifetime value, campaign cost, optimal spend per channel, seasonality, etc.

CHAPTER 2

LIFETIME VALUE FRAMEWORK

*The time has come when advertising has in some hands
reached the status of a science. It is based on fixed
principles and is reasonably exact. The causes and effects
have been analyzed until they are well understood.*

*The correct methods of procedure have been
proved and established. We know what is
most effective, and we act on basic law.*

*Advertising, once a gamble, has thus become, under
able direction, one of the safest business ventures.*

—CLAUDE HOPKINS, *Scientific Advertising,* 1923[1]

In the previous chapter, we discussed the first tactic of the Five-Tactic
Marketing Framework: brand and performance marketing. We evaluated
the individual strengths of each and discovered how much more powerful they can be when implemented together. We also learned how to
amplify their combined power through the application of AI tools (tactic
#5). But none of that learning's going to do us any good if we don't have
the money to implement it. This is where tactic #2 comes in.

Most companies run brand and performance marketing on an inflex-
ible budget. They've got some fixed amount that they can spend per
quarter, per year, or per campaign. While this approach might work in
some cases, it's almost always going to return sub-optimal results. If you

want to maximize efficiency and optimize your marketing spend, you don't want to use a budget. Instead, you want to use profitability metrics. This chapter will show you how to use the second tactic of SMB marketing, which I call the "Lifetime Value Framework."

The Lifetime Value Framework (LVF) uses a well-known concept, customer lifetime value (CLV), to calculate how much total revenue any given customer brings into your business. Based on that number, the LVF reverse engineers a maximum allowable marketing spend for each stage of the funnel. It's a five-step process that optimizes our marketing efforts, ensuring that we're never operating beyond our means or below our capacity. Here are the five steps at a glance:

- Step 1: Calculate CLV (customer lifetime value)
  Determine the average lifetime revenue per customer.

- Step 2: CLV ® CAC Allowable (customer acquisition cost)
  Based on the average lifetime revenue, determine how much you can pay to acquire each new customer. This is the pot of money you can spend across the entire funnel. For our purposes here, if our goal is break even on the initial acquisition of the customer, this number is equal to the average lifetime profit per customer.

- Step 3: CAC ® CPM Allowable (cost per thousand impressions)
  Based on the allowable cost to acquire each new customer, determine how much you can spend generating each new impression.

- Step 4: CAC ® CPL Allowable (cost per lead)
  Based on the allowable cost to acquire each new customer, determine how much you can spend generating each new lead.

- Step 5: CAC ® CPA Allowable (cost per acquisition)
  Based on the allowable cost to acquire each new customer, determine how much you can spend converting leads into customers.

Working through the five-step Lifetime Value Framework shifts us into a self-sustaining financial model that requires no third-party investors. Every impression, lead, and conversion is paid for using the profits from prior sales.

Simultaneously, the LVF frees us from the chains of traditional marketing budgets, ensuring that every campaign is given the opportunity to run at maximum power while remaining profitable. For each stage of the funnel, the LVF gives us a maximum allowable spend. These allowables are calculated to ensure absolute optimization. Whereas budget-based marketing often allocates resources arbitrarily and leaves much to chance, the LVF guarantees two things: we never overspend (which would cut into our profits) and never underspend (which would leave money on the table). We always break even or come out ahead. Performance marketing at its finest.

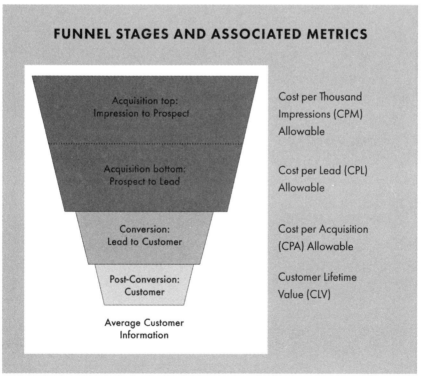

FUNNEL STAGES AND ASSOCIATED METRICS

Acquisition top:
Impression to Prospect

Cost per Thousand
Impressions (CPM)
Allowable

Acquisition bottom:
Prospect to Lead

Cost per Lead (CPL)
Allowable

Conversion:
Lead to Customer

Cost per Acquisition
(CPA) Allowable

Post-Conversion:
Customer

Customer Lifetime
Value (CLV)

Average Customer
Information

continued

Funnel stages and the associated allowables:

Acquisition (Top)

- **Goal:** Targeted exposure

- **Metric:** Impressions

- **Allowable:** CPM (cost per thousand impressions)

- *Get in front of your target audience so that they are familiar with your brand. Begin to build recognition of your brand identity and value. This exposure will help build trust and hopefully result in lead generation.*

Acquisition (Bottom)

- **Goal:** Lead generation

- **Metric:** Lead conversion rate

- **Allowable:** CPL (cost per lead)

- *Turn impressions into leads. Gather information on prospective customers in exchange for value. This information can then be used to inform/enable additional marketing with the goal of turning leads into customers.*

Conversion

- **Goal:** Conversion

- **Metric:** Customer conversion rate

- **Allowable:** CPA (cost per acquisition)

- *Turn leads into customers. Use targeted marketing of products and services to grow your customer base.*

Post-Conversion

- **Goal:** Increase the average value of a customer

- **Metric:** Revenue

- **Allowable:** N/A. Post-conversion returns are reflected by CLV (customer lifetime value)

- *Use retention, cross-sell/upsell in order to make the average customer more profitable.*

Consider this: the drivers in the Indianapolis 500 are remarkably skilled. The Indianapolis Motor Speedway track has four corners, and during the race, the cars complete 200 laps. To win, the drivers have to take 800 corners at over 200 miles per hour in about 3 hours while driving just a few feet—sometimes just a few inches—from 32 other drivers going just as fast. They come out of those turns about 18 inches from the wall, turn after turn. They are barely out of one corner before they have to start into the next one. If they slow down and don't push their cars to the limit in the corners, they won't have a chance to win. If they go too fast or don't hit a corner perfectly, they'll hit the wall. They can't take a "that's good enough" approach.

Similarly, you can use the Lifetime Value Framework to push your performance program right up to, but not over, the limit of profitability. Frankly, most companies don't do this; most take a "good enough" budget-based approach. As a result, they are leaving money on the table. Lots of it.

NEVER LEAVE MONEY ON THE TABLE

Imagine that there's a casino with a unique coin flip game. You pay $10 to flip a coin. If it's heads, you win $120. If it's tails, you owe them $80. The coin is fair; it's not weighted in any way to make it come up tails more than heads. Half of the time it will be heads, and half of the time it will be tails. For every two flips, you'll average a $20 profit—$10 per flip. Sure, occasionally you'll go on a run with a couple or even several heads or tails in a row, but even in the short run, it's rarely far off from 50/50.

Let's say that you flip the coin every five seconds. In a minute, you'd flip it 12 times and make $120. Nice! In 10 minutes, you'd make $1,200. Amazing! In an hour $7,200. Sign me up!

Now, if a casino was stupid enough to offer this game, you'd play it until you physically couldn't flip any more coins. When your fingers got too tired, you'd be flipping with your elbows, with your toes, to make $7,200 an hour. You wouldn't say, "I'm budgeting $250 for the coin flip game. Once I've spent my $250, regardless of how much I win, I'm going to stop." But that's what companies do all the time.

It's very common for companies that have successful, profitable performance programs to say, "Our budget for this year will be $XXX,XXX dollars" even though the program is so highly profitable that it's self-sustaining. They put a ceiling on their success. They could reinvest the profits from performance marketing back into new or existing programs to generate more and more sales and profits until they maxed out the channel or campaign, but few companies choose to do so.

But outperformers do. Outperformers know that by putting more into a profitable program that is paying for itself they can be even more profitable. And it doesn't cost them anything—essentially, they're playing with "house money"—because they've generated the sales and profits to fuel it. Count me in!

IS THIS REALLY PROFITABLE?

Some people who don't understand the Lifetime Value Framework think that it can't be profitable, that you're burning all your profits chasing after those last sales. But that's wrong.

You're never reducing your profits because every incremental sale is profitable. It is true that the last sales will be at a lower profit than the easier initial sales, but they're all adding dollars to your company's bottom line. And when they stop being profitable, that is when you dial back your program to the point where they are profitable again.

When Edwin Drake drilled the first oil well in 1859, he only had to go down 69 feet to hit a pocket of oil that immediately started producing 25 barrels a day—a big deal at the time.

Today, oil companies may spend billions of dollars drilling wells that are sometimes tens of thousands of feet deep to find oil. They take more work and cost way more, but they're still profitable.

It is an unfortunate fact of marketing that once you have maximized results from a certain channel or campaign, you must move to the next most efficient medium or channel. However, without the LVF we may be moving to that new medium or channel while still leaving potential sales on the table in the medium and channels we are already operating in. The LVF helps to ensure that we make the most of every opportunity.

BREAKING EVEN AND TURNING PROFITS

In its most basic form, the Lifetime Value Framework is designed to ensure that we break even on customer acquisition. Every dollar that an average customer gives us is earmarked toward bringing a new customer into the fold. If the average customer results in $100 in profit, then we're going to spend $100 bringing in each new customer. As we've already established, this break-even approach ensures that we neither underspend nor overspend, maximizing our growth without leaving us overleveraged.

The question then arises—if the LVF is designed to ensure that we break even, how do we transcend the LVF to turn a profit?

The answer's simple: increase lifetime value. We'll turn a profit on post-conversion. Once a customer comes into the fold, we must do everything we can to earn renewal, upsell, or cross-sell.

Think of loss leaders in retail shops. The loss-leading product is unprofitable to sell, but we know that once customers are in the door, they'll buy something else of greater value. As retailers, we're interested in the total value of the cart, not just the value of our loss leader. We dip into the red for our loss leader, then turn a profit on the rest of the cart.

Same concept here. We may break even on the initial conversion, but the long-term economics should be extremely profitable.

It's worth noting that this is harder to pull off in retail or "one and done" type engagements, where the lion's share of value is exchanged during the initial conversion. But in B2B sales, the product is usually much stickier. Customer lifetimes extend far beyond the initial conversion, and value grows dramatically over time. It's precisely these sorts of businesses that have the most to gain by executing a break-even strategy during customer acquisition.

It's also important to understand that this break-even approach represents just one way of executing on the LVF. It's the simplest approach, so it's the one we'll focus on here. But we'll take a glance at some alternatives shortly.

Finally, one last caveat on this topic: in this chapter, we're going to focus exclusively on funnel spending. Obviously, you'll spend additional dollars post-funnel, as you upsell, cross-sell, and promote renewals. But those allowables are a topic for another time. Here, we're interested exclusively in resource allocation for acquisition and conversion.

STEP 1: CALCULATING THE CUSTOMER LIFETIME VALUE (CLV)

All right. So we've established that the Lifetime Value Framework is indeed profitable. We've also established that we need the LVF in order to ensure that we're spending well—neither leaving money on the table nor writing checks we can't cash. But how does the LVF actually work?

To start using the framework, we first need to calculate CLV. This metric, the average revenue generated by a customer, will then help inform all the allowables that populate the framework.

CLV can be calculated in a number of ways, but for the purposes of this book, we will use the following formula:

CLV = average duration that customer buys from company × average order frequency per period × average order value

- Average duration—This is the average time frame a business retains a customer. Depending on the type of product sold, it could be days, weeks, months, or years.

- Average order frequency per period—This is the average number of times a customer buys within a fixed period, such as a day, week, month, quarter, or year. (Select the interval that suits your business best.)

- Average order value—The average price of an order.

So, for example, if the average customer does business with the company for five years and buys two times per year with an average order of $1,000, we would calculate that CLV as:

$$5 \times 2 \times \$1{,}000 = \$10{,}000 \text{ CLV}$$

While this method for determining CLV seems straightforward enough—even simple—in practice, it can be very complex. Each part of that formula can be challenging for many companies to determine. While more than three-quarters of businesspeople in a survey said that they think CLV is important, only 11% strongly agreed that they could measure it.[2]

Indeed, in my experience, few small and mid-sized companies are accurately measuring CLV. And without an idea of your CLV, you can't use the Lifetime Value Framework.

What is stopping companies from measuring CLV?

It would be easy to measure CLV if you only had one product sold via one channel at one price and level of profit. And if you have good data. But this is rarely the case.

Many companies have dozens or hundreds, if not thousands, of products. They are sold via various channels at different profit margins. The people and companies buying them may be very different. For example, a consumer buying at Home Depot is going to have a very different CLV than a contractor buying there.

And then there's that word "average." This can be difficult to calculate in many businesses, where averages vary wildly across different customer segments. In *How Brands Grow*, Byron Sharp shows that for most companies, from Coca-Cola to Apple, their buyers fall along a classic "long-tail" pattern with a few heavy, repeat buyers and many occasional light buyers. This is even more exaggerated in most B2B cases.[3]

The following graph illustrates this concept, charting the number of customers along the x-axis and the average order value along the y-axis. As you can see, there are far more customers with a lower average order value (point B) than there are customers with a higher average order value (point A).

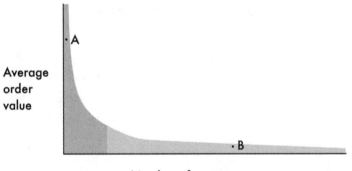

Number of customers

If your company has a similar pattern, and most do, a new heavy buyer is worth a lot more than a new light buyer, but you need both. Your "average" customer may be halfway down that curve.

The average duration that a company retains a customer may spread out along a bell curve, too, with some buying from you just once and others becoming repeat customers for years.

This is all by way of saying that one major obstacle to calculating CLV may be defining your "average" and accounting for variance. It often takes serious work to arrive at a single, weighted figure that reflects all products, channels, and buyer types.

Having said that, the core challenge in calculating your CLV may be about something else entirely: it may be about the data itself. In many companies, not all data is collected, it may be siloed, or it may be inaccurately reported. The company may not have a single point of truth. And if you don't have access to accurate, reliable numbers, it's very hard to calculate CLV. Garbage in, garbage out.

It's surprising how often a "bad data" problem is actually a bad *reporting* problem. This happens when departments misrepresent the facts in order to cast their performance in a more favorable light. Whenever an issue like this arises, I always think back to Ford:

> When Alan Mulally was CEO of Ford during the financial crisis of '08, the company had to report an annual loss of $14.6 billion. It wasn't at all clear that Ford would even survive the crisis. Sometime during that period, he called a meeting of all the unit heads worldwide, asking them all to report their status.
>
> One by one, the senior execs gave their reports, painting a rosy picture. Everything was going great in my department, thank you, sir. Do you need any help? Nope, no help needed here. One by one, dozens of them, in turn, declared their dashboard status green.
>
> After several instances of rosy status reports, Mulally called the meeting to a halt and asked a simple question: If everything is so great, then how come I just had to report to the public that we lost 14 billion dollars?[4]

Point is: data malfunctions happen to the best of us. Even so, you shouldn't let problems like these hold you back. For the purposes of your performance marketing efforts, simpler may very well be better. You may not need your company's customer lifetime value figure; you may only need the CLV for the product(s) or market segment(s) on which your company is focused.

Avoid analysis paralysis. Sit down with the company's senior executives, use the best data that you have, and make a decision on CLV that you can live and work with.

A key driver of Amazon's success is their willingness to act on partial data. "You want to encourage your leaders and employees to act with only about 70% of the data they wish they had—waiting for 90% or more means you are likely moving too slow," writes Daniel Slater, the AWS Worldwide lead of culture innovation.[5] Be like Amazon.

STEP 2: CALCULATING THE CUSTOMER ACQUISITION COST (CAC) ALLOWABLE

Once we have determined customer lifetime value (CLV), the next step is to use it to determine the customer acquisition cost (CAC) allowable. This will represent the total dollar amount we can spend to break even in the acquisition of a new customer, from impression to conversion.

Unlike traditional marketers, we're not going to derive this allowable from an arbitrary budget. Instead, we're going to look at the lifetime value of our average customer and use that figure to reverse engineer an acceptable spend per acquisition. Doing so will help us ensure that we're both never leaving money on the table and never spending marketing dollars that we don't have.

As with CLV, there are numerous ways to calculate CAC, but for the purposes of this book, we will use this formula:

CAC allowable = CLV × average net margin

- CLV—customer lifetime value, as derived earlier

- Average net margin—the average net margin overall of the product or business line for which you are performing the calculation

Said another way, this amount is the average profitability per customer. This means that if we were to spend an amount equal to this to acquire a new customer, and that customer turns out to be average, we would break even on that acquisition. If we spend more than the CAC allowable to acquire a new customer, we risk that customer being unprofitable.

It should be noted that CAC is a holistic business metric that is not campaign specific. The CAC allowable applies to all sales and marketing efforts over a certain period of time. (We get into campaign-specific metrics in the next section.)

To continue our example, in order to calculate CLV, we need the average net margin of the business. If the average net margin is 50%, our equation looks like this:

CAC allowable: $10,000 × .5 = $5,000

Sounds simple, right?

Well, mostly it is. But, as with the calculation of CLV, we do have to ensure that the data correctly represents the product or business line we are attempting to calculate for.

Don't underestimate the value of a "gut check" with these calculations. Do the numbers we are using in the formulas check out using common sense? Do the results of the formulas make sense given the context of the business? For example, if your business sells industrial manufacturing equipment and the lowest cost of a machine is $50,000 with an average net margin of 10%, it is very unlikely that your CAC allowable will be less than $5,000.

Performance, Allowable, and Projection Metrics

Note that we are calculating the CAC *allowable* in this section, not the current CAC. Calculating the current CAC will give you an understanding of how much your business is spending today to acquire a customer. Our goal is different in that we are attempting to understand what we *should* be spending. We're trying to find the number that will maximize our yield without exceeding our income.

That being said, it is a great idea (read: imperative) to compare the CAC allowable and the current overall CAC. This will give you an idea of how the business is performing in relation to the overall cost of acquiring customers.

It will be important to apply this general principle across the entire Lifetime Value Framework: there can be big differences between performance, allowable, and projection numbers. We have to use the right number in the right place and keep a close eye on what the differences between these numbers are.

"Performance" metrics measure what your business looks like *today*. How much are you currently spending to acquire each customer? How much are you currently spending on impressions? On leads? On conversion?

"Allowables" measure how much you *could* safely spend. Ideally, you want your allowable and performance numbers to be the same, but they often won't be. If your current performance metrics are higher than your allowables, it means that today's actual real-world spend is too high. (You're spending $1,000, but you're only allowed to spend $500.) If your current performance metrics are lower than your allowables, it means that you're spending less than you could be. You're missing an opportunity to maximize marketing efforts. (You're spending $1,000, but you're allowed to spend $5,000.)

Finally, we've got "projections." These are hypothetical calculations of what your numbers *would* look like in some alternative scenario.

When setting an allowable for immediate implementation, you always want to calculate it using today's real-world performance metrics. Otherwise, you might end up spending money that you don't have.

Alternatives to the Break-Even Model

As we established earlier, this book will focus on a break-even application of the Lifetime Value Framework. We're looking to maximize our performance by maximizing our spend, while never straying into the red. Our goal is to give the funnel every dollar that we can afford—no more, no less. And we'll turn our profit later, when we grow customer lifetime value post-funnel.

But it's important to note that there are alternatives to the break-even model. You can make your CAC allowable anything you'd like—profitable or unprofitable. Some businesses may want to increase profitability by setting their CAC allowable below their current CLV. Meanwhile, others may want to spend a sum greater than their current CLV.

For instance, a small business that needs to ensure profitability might not pursue growth as aggressively. They'd spend less than they're taking in, thereby guaranteeing profitability on day 1. Which is to say that they'd want a CAC allowable below their CLV.

On the other hand, a VC-funded business may need to grow at all costs—profitability be damned. As a consequence, they might set their allowable CAC far above their current CLV, ensuring rapid scaling even if it requires spending money that they can't reliably earn back from customers.

Having said all that, this book will continue to work with the break-even model because it best illustrates the optimizing power of the Lifetime Value Framework.

STEP 3: CALCULATING THE COST PER THOUSAND IMPRESSIONS (CPM) ALLOWABLE

So far, the figures for customer lifetime value (CLV) and the customer acquisition cost (CAC) allowable have helped us determine the lifetime profitability of a customer. And, by extension, they've revealed how much we can spend on each customer across the entire span of the funnel's acquisition and conversion phases. Now it's time to determine what we can spend at each individual stage of the funnel. Namely, we need to determine how the CAC allowable pot gets split across impressions, leads, and acquisitions.

We're going to begin by calculating our allowable CPM—cost per thousand impressions. This is the amount we can afford to pay when attracting new eyeballs to our brand or product.

Like the other allowables to come, this one represents a slice of available CAC funds. So we'll calculate it by multiplying the CAC allowable times our average impression conversion rate. This will ensure that our spend for impressions is proportionate to the value of those impressions.

(Incidentally, this is called the "direct method" of value determination because it uses historic business data—"performance metrics"—to inform decision-making, as opposed to using projections.)

The formula looks like this:

CPM allowable = CAC allowable × average impression conversion rate

- CAC allowable—our allowable customer acquisition cost as derived earlier

- Average impression conversion rate—the average conversion rate of impressions to leads

To illustrate what this looks like in practice, let's refer back to our example from earlier. We previously set our CAC allowable at $5,000. Now let's say our average impression conversion rate is 2%. That would mean our CPM allowable is calculated as:

$5,000 × 2% = $100

This equation tells us that we can spend up to $100 per thousand impressions and still remain profitable from a customer acquisition standpoint, as long as our impression-to-lead conversion rates remain consistent.

I have mentioned repeatedly that a business must move continuously to the next most efficient medium—impression-based marketing is a great example of this. As you are probably aware, this is the "least qualified" audience in that they have not shown any intent and have satisfied only our most limited targeting parameters. The unqualified, inactionable character of impressions is reflected in their cost. Billboards, display banner advertising, banners at tradeshows or events—this marketing will be cheap, but the majority of its audience will be either unqualified, unable to act, or a combination of the two.

This doesn't necessarily mean that impression-based marketing is a waste of money! Depending on your metrics and the type of business you're in, these may be wonderful opportunities. There's a reason why the average Super Bowl ad costs millions of dollars.

Putting Our CPM Allowable into Practice

Earlier, I suggested that you should always be monitoring the gap between your current performance metrics and your allowables. If today's performance costs exceed your allowables, it means you're overspending. If today's performance costs fall short of your allowables, then it means you're underspending. Namely, you're leaving money on the table.

Let's see how this would play out given our existing example. A moment ago, we used our CAC allowable and current impression conversion rate to set our CPM allowable at $100. Now let's imagine that we have an impression-generation campaign with the following data points on a monthly basis:

Monthly media spend (billboards + local sponsorships): $100,000
Impressions generated: 1,010,101

This campaign is generating 1,010,101 impressions per month at a CPM of $99.

$100,000/1,010,101 x 1,000 = $99 CPM

Given that our allowable CPM is $100, we are right on the money! We can continue to spend this amount as long as impression-to-lead conversion rates hold steady.

Note: this is probably the trickiest of all stages to calculate—the reason being that a lot of the campaigns at this stage might be brand based rather than performance based. They might not be designed to lead directly to leads or conversions but contribute to "incremental lift" across all other efforts. More on this in Chapter 5.

(Incremental lift is a topic we will not dive into in this book, but if you are interested, check out the blog *Occam's Razor* by Avinash Kaushik.[6])

STEP 4: CALCULATING THE COST PER LEAD (CPL) ALLOWABLE

So far, we've calculated our customer lifetime value (CLV) and our allowable customer acquisition cost (CAC) in order to determine precisely how much money we can afford to spend on each customer's journey through the funnel. Then, in the previous section, we considered the top of the acquisition stage of the funnel—impressions—and calculated our allowable spend for that chapter in the customer's journey. Now it's time to move further down the funnel.

Up next: lead gen. We need to determine how much we can afford to pay for each lead.

To understand our allowable cost per lead (CPL), we once again need to go back to our customer acquisition cost allowable. That's the total pot of money we have to play with across all of our funnel marketing efforts.

Then, we have to subtract the money that we're allowed to spend on impressions—our allowable CPM.

Finally, we'll multiply that total by our current average lead conversion rate. As with impressions, we use this "direct method" of calculation to ensure that our spend per lead is commensurate to that lead's value.

Here's the formula:

**CPL allowable = (CAC allowable – CPM allowable) ×
average lead conversion rate**

- CAC allowable—our allowable customer acquisition cost as derived earlier

- CPM allowable—our allowable cost per thousand impressions as derived earlier

- Average lead conversion rate—the average conversion rate of leads to customers

Back to our example. Earlier, we calculated that our CAC allowable was $5,000, and our CPM allowable was $100. Now let's say our average lead conversion rate is 10%. That would mean our CPL allowable is calculated as:

($5,000 – $100) × 10% = $490

This equation tells us that we can spend up to $490 per lead and still remain profitable from a customer acquisition standpoint, as long as our lead-to-conversion rates remain consistent.

Why is this important? Because quality lead generation is not only extremely important, but it is also extremely difficult! Getting in front of the right audience, at the right time, with the right offer is critical to building a database of qualified potential customers.

Given both the difficulty and importance of lead generation, it's imperative that we give it every available dollar—stopping short only of breaking the bank and/or bankrupting the other funnel stages.

Here's the trouble: many businesses don't want to spend every available dollar. They only want to spend on their top-tier, most efficient lead-gen channels. Once those channels are maxed out, these businesses stop spending. And that's a huge mistake. That's where the failure to maximize and optimize begins. If you have more dollars to spend on lead gen, you should spend them. Your most efficient channel might be maxed out, but you can always move to the *next* most efficient channel.

As we discussed earlier, when a business matures, it becomes increasingly difficult to find that next customer or lead. But this is not a cue to stop spending. Just as with our oil well example, a business must move to the next most efficient medium for both lead generation and new customer conversion. Efficiency will drop, but as long as you're still spending within your CPL allowable, you're safe.

If you don't keep spending up to your allowable, nothing terrible will happen today. But over time, you'll see sales plateau, experience business stagnation, and risk losing ground to competitors.

Putting Our CPL into Practice

As we discussed earlier, it's important to keep an eye on the difference between our allowables and our current performance metrics. So let's expand on our example. Let's say we are currently running a lead generation campaign with the following data points on a monthly basis:

Monthly media spend (social media + display campaigns + affiliate marketing): $450,000

Leads generated: 1,000

This campaign is generating 1,000 new leads per month at a performance CPL of $450.

$450,000 / 1,000 leads = $450 CPL

Given that our allowable CPL is $490, we are approaching, but not over the limit of spend on this campaign. We can afford to increase spending incrementally, perhaps starting with the channels that have the highest conversion rates, until we reach our CPL allowable.

Fine-Tuning Your CPL

Note that your allowable cost per lead may vary based on product, segment, marketing channel, and other factors. And you should always be tweaking the dials to get the most from your lead generation campaigns, including testing new channels, initiatives, etc.

One surefire way to decrease CPL is to increase acquisition stage campaign conversion rates. The higher the lead conversion rates, the more effective the campaigns (duh), and the more financial and other resources you can dedicate to them. More on this in Chapter 5.

STEP 5: CALCULATING THE COST PER ACQUISITION (CPA) ALLOWABLE

Last step!

With impressions and leads behind us, we're going to wrap up by calculating our allowable CPA. This is the amount we can afford to pay when converting a lead into a customer.

Like the other allowables, this one represents a slice of available CAC funds, so it will need to factor in the spending on previous funnel stages. We're going to take the allowable CAC and subtract out dollars that we've already allocated for impressions and leads. What remains will be our allowable conversion spend.

So for the purposes of this book, we will use this equation:

CPA allowable = CAC allowable − (CPL allowable + CPM allowable)

- CAC allowable—our allowable customer acquisition cost as derived earlier

- CPL allowable—our allowable cost per lead as derived earlier

- CPM allowable—our allowable cost per thousand impressions as derived earlier

This is where things can get a bit tricky. There will be multiple instances where the CPA allowable can and should equal the CAC allowable (minus impression costs, where applicable). This will be specific to channels where a customer is able to go straight from impression to conversion, skipping the lead generation stage altogether. (In these cases, the cost per lead is $0.)

A good example is transactional keyword-based paid search ("pay per click" or "PPC" campaigns). The goal of these campaigns is to identify and convert customers searching for purchase intent–based keywords. These might include words such as "cheapest," "fastest," "buy XXXX online," etc. In "transaction-based" PPC campaigns, your CPA allowable should be equal to your CAC allowable as it will enable you to acquire as many customers via that channel as possible.

Unlike the CAC allowable, the CPA allowable is a campaign-specific metric. It is designed to tell us the upper limit of what we can spend per campaign to convert a lead to a customer. It should be applied on a campaign-by-campaign basis.

And while both CAC and CPA are ostensibly "acquisition" allowables, it's important to understand that they interact with the funnel very differently. Our allowable CAC governs spending across the entire acquisition section of the funnel, from impressions through conversions. By contrast, the allowable CPA specifically governs the conversion phase of the funnel, where we transform leads into customers. Put another way, the CPA is one of a few costs, which, when taken together, should add up to our total CAC allowable.

Let's continue with our earlier example using two different campaigns, one that is straight from impression to conversion and one that has a lead source.

Campaign #1: Straight to Conversion

As there is no cost for the lead generation element with this campaign, the calculation of the cost per acquisition allowable will look like this:

$5,000 CAC allowable – ($0 CPL + $0 CPM) = $5,000

This means that we are able to spend the full amount of our allowable customer acquisition cost when calculating CPA for this campaign.

Some who are very familiar with pay per click may say, "What about the cost of the click?" Great question! Since the campaign is purely transaction based, the cost of the click is baked into the conversion rate.

For example, say we have a PPC campaign with a spend of $100,000 per month that is generating 1,000 customers within that time period. That campaign is generating 1,000 new customers at a CPA of $100.

$100,000 / 1,000 customers = $100 CPA

The CPA is inclusive of spends on clicks and still is nowhere near our allowable CPA of $5,000! Depending on how steeply conversion rates drop when we increase spend, we can afford to put a lot more financial resources behind this campaign in order to approach our profitability threshold.

Campaign #2: Lead Sourced

For this campaign, let's return to the allowables examples that we calculated earlier. Our total pot of money (or our CAC allowable) is $5,000. And we've already allocated $100 to spend on impressions (our CPM allowable) as well as $490 to spend on leads (our CPL allowable). This would mean our CPA allowable calculation would look something like this:

$5,000 – ($490 + $100) = $4,410

This means we can spend up to $4,410 when attempting to convert the leads we have acquired into customers.

To use a nurture campaign–based example, let's say we have a conversion-based campaign that has the following data points on a monthly basis.

Monthly media spend
(social media + direct mail + email platform): $800,000

Leads in the campaign: 1,000

Conversion rate: 10%

This campaign is generating 100 new customers a month at a CPA of $8,000.

1,000 leads × 10% = 100 new customers

$800,000/100 customers = $8,000 CPA

Given that our allowable CPA is only $4,410, we are grossly overspending on this campaign if we want to remain profitable. We need to examine the various elements of this campaign in order to either increase conversion rates or lower CPA.

Fine-Tuning Your CPA

The allowable cost per acquisition may vary considerably based on product, segment, marketing channel, and other factors.

Also note that, as with CPL, you should always be tweaking the dials to get the most from your conversion campaigns, including adding new creative when your creative becomes exhausted. One surefire way to decrease CPA is to increase conversion-stage campaign conversion rates. The higher the conversion rates, the more effective the campaigns (once again, duh), and the more financial and other resources you can dedicate to them. More on this in Chapter 6.

CONNECTING THE METRICS

With the Lifetime Value Framework (LVF), if you're producing customers in the conversion stage at less than the allowable cost per acquisition (CPA), you can increase your spend up to the allowable and produce even more! As long as your conversion rate doesn't decrease, you'll produce more new profitable customers.

Similarly, if you're converting leads at less than the allowable cost per lead (CPL), you can spend more to get more qualified leads.

The same applies for impressions to leads, governed by the cost per thousand impressions (CPM) allowable.

With LVF, you know these numbers and can adjust the dials to not just meet but possibly exceed your goals for sales and profits.

It sounds simple: if you're under the stage-specific allowable, increase your campaigns' spend to maximize results. If you're exceeding your allowables, decrease spend to stay profitable.

But things in business are never that easy.

In Chapters 5, 6, and 7, I do a deeper dive into how to use the Lifetime Value Framework, combining it with the other four marketing tactics to maximize results across the acquisition, conversion, and customer retention stages.

Remember: if you're not maximizing results, you're leaving money on the table.

FLIP THE FUNNEL

Throughout this chapter, we've focused on calculating our acquisition allowables. To do that math, we've followed the funnel's traditional trajectory top-to-bottom—what you might call the funnel's natural "gravity." First, we calculated spending for impressions, then we moved down to leads, and then we moved down to conversion.

But it's important to understand that the laws of funnel gravity don't always apply. Outperformers intentionally break the laws of funnel gravity during implementation. Their math continues to flow top-to-bottom, and their prospects continue to flow top-to-bottom, but their campaigns flow bottom-to-top.

This is to say that when you're overhauling and/or optimizing your business's marketing strategy, you don't want to start at the top of the funnel with impressions. Instead, you want to start at the bottom.

First things first; work on your post-conversion: look for ways to get more value out of current customers. Upsell, cross-sell, and promote renewals. This is perhaps the most powerful thing you can do to drive up CLV, giving you more money to play with at every stage of the funnel.

Only after you've begun optimizing post-conversion efforts should you then work your way up to conversion, improving the lead-to-customer journey. The higher you get your conversion rates here, the more money you can justify spending on impressions and lead generation.

With post-conversion and conversion accounted for, you'll finally be ready to move up to the top of the funnel, improving leads, impressions, and impression-to-lead rates.

You might think of it this way: when customers interact with the funnel, they see it from the top down. When budgeters interact with the funnel, they see it the same way. But when marketers operationalize funnel campaigns, they need to "flip the funnel" and take a bottom-to-top approach.

— *SIDEBAR* —

CALCULATING THE LIFETIME VALUE FRAMEWORK'S ALLOWABLES

CLV = average duration that customer buys from company × average order frequency per period × average order value

CAC allowable = CLV × average net margin

CPM allowable = CAC allowable × average impression conversion rate

CPL allowable = (CAC allowable – CPM allowable) × average lead conversion rate

CPA allowable = CAC allowable - (CPL allowable + CPM allowable)

A FEW FINAL DETAILS

We've now finished a complete overview of the second tactic in SMB marketing: the Lifetime Value Framework. But before we move on, it's important to cover a few last details about the LVF.

Campaign Time Frames and Other Relevant Considerations

Many of your performance campaigns will be digital. And many of us expect digital programs to have rapid results. But the Lifetime Value Framework requires patience.

The US Navy SEALs are known for their saying "Slow is smooth, smooth is fast." These teams are methodical and patient in planning and executing time-critical missions. They have learned in crisis situations that working at a slow and smooth pace reduces mistakes and, in the end, speeds *up* the mission.[7]

Generally speaking, the time frame for selling your products will determine the time frame for seeing LVF results. If you're selling a low-cost item that people typically make a quick decision about—almost an impulse purchase—you should expect quicker results. People won't be in the acquisition and conversion phases for very long. But if you're selling a more expensive item with a more complex decision-making process, with multiple people on the buying team, and you know from history that it can take months for a decision to be made, then don't expect your new performance-generated leads to close any faster.

For most deals, you may need 18 months to be able to fully test and evaluate your program. For five- and six-figure deals, you may need even longer. In the first few months, you'll be generating leads and optimizing the conversion phase, but you won't have many sales to prove ultimate success. For the program to succeed, you and your C-suite will need to agree to it in advance.[8] You'll need to have the patience to stay the course.

Here are a couple of other considerations when working with the Lifetime Value Framework.

First: CLV. You have the ability to bend the curve—to increase your customer lifetime value—which will ripple up through the program, allowing you to spend more at each stage of the marketing funnel. It's a fairly simple concept: the more the average customer is worth to the business, the more you can spend on marketing to acquire new customers. You increase CLV by improving your customer experience, actively engaging with your customers to resubscribe or buy more. We talk more about this later, but some ideas include adding unique value that customers want but that you wouldn't offer to prospects, increasing prices and margins as your brand strength grows, cross-selling, upselling, etc.

Next: CAC. There are multiple ways that companies calculate overall customer acquisition cost. Do your research before you make a back-of-the-napkin calculation. As discussed earlier, this is a holistic business metric—meaning that it must take into account salaries, commissions, tools, etc.

Also, be sure not to confuse CAC (customer acquisition cost) and CPA (cost per acquisition). As discussed, CPA is a campaign-specific metric, and it exclusively governs the narrow funnel region devoted to conversion. By contrast, CAC represents the all-in cost of customer acquisition from impression through conversion.

Finally, another application in which CAC can be useful is understanding fully loaded costs when considering entering a new market. For many industries, CLV needs to be three times CAC for the business to be profitable. If CLV-to-CAC is lower than that, you may not be profitable. If it's much higher than that, you may be underinvesting in marketing that could bring in profitable customers. But these ratios may be different in your industry.[9]

In Chapters 5, 6, and 7, I do a deeper dive into how to use the Lifetime Value Framework to maximize results in the acquisition, conversion, and customer retention stages. If you're not maximizing results, you're leaving money on the table.

CASE STUDY—GET LVF FIT

In addition to consulting companies on their e-commerce programs, I have also launched and operated my own e-commerce businesses. My clients, of course, can decide how they want to run their programs and whether they are going to fully embrace the Lifetime Value Framework. For my own companies, though, I'm not interested in average or "acceptable" profits; I want to outperform the competition. I want to realize every possible dollar of profit.

In 2019, we created the Insure Fitness Group to sell professional liability insurance to fitness instructors and personal trainers. After being successful with those solopreneurs, we expanded to dance instructors, spin instructors, boot camp instructors, and other similar professionals.

In his 1985 classic, *Ogilvy on Advertising*, David Ogilvy wrote, "You aren't advertising to a standing army; you are advertising to a moving parade. The advertisement which sold a refrigerator to couples who got married last year will probably be just as successful with couples who get married this year."[10] Ogilvy's insight certainly applies to this market.

The typical fitness instructor is only in the market for about two years, so churn is huge. We need to constantly be landing new customers. But the price of the insurance is often around \$250/year (I'm using approximate numbers here). With such a low-cost item for such a short period of time, the customer lifetime value (CLV) is roughly \$500.

**CLV = average duration that customer buys from company ×
average order frequency per period × average order value**

CLV = 2 years × 1 order per year × \$250 = \$500

Across all the professions that we were targeting, though, there could be over one million people at any one time—Ogilvy's moving parade. The opportunity was there. We could build a profitable business just as long as we could keep our all-in full-funnel per-customer costs down.

That all-in number is our allowable customer acquisition cost (CAC). Since we were following this book's break-even model, the essential task was to identify how much of each customer's lifetime value was profit and then allocate those dollars toward marketing. If we estimate a 20% margin, then the formula would look something like this:

CAC allowable = CLV × average net margin
CAC allowable = \$500 × 20% = \$100

While the target market was viable and the CAC allowable was workable, we faced significant challenges when we launched Insure Fitness Group. First, this market was highly saturated with extremely well-funded, venture-backed organizations. Second, there is no licensure requirement for the type of work these individuals do, meaning there are no official databases or contact lists to pull from. And finally, again, the CLV is quite low. So, it was imperative to find low-cost, highly efficient means of marketing in order to be profitable.

Although paid search advertising is often one of the best if not *the* best performance channel for my companies and clients, it wasn't available to us in this market because those VC-funded competitors had irrationally bid up the cost per click of relevant keywords to absurd levels: $40/click or more. They were losing money on every paid search–generated deal. (But I am sure they made it up with volume . . .)

While paid search advertising is not a "pure" impressions play, thinking of it in those terms will help reveal why $40/click was such an unreasonable number. You'll recall that our allowable spend per thousand impressions (CPM) is calculated by multiplying the CAC allowable by the average impression conversion rate. If we estimate that the conversion rate was about 1%, then here's what the allowable would look like:

CPM allowable = CAC allowable × average impression conversion rate
CPM allowable = $100 × 1% = $1

So a bold, break-even spend in this scenario would be $1 for every thousand impressions. But our VC-funded competitors were paying $40 per click. Yikes!

Email is typically another low-cost, sure-fire channel, but—again—not this time. These instructors do not need to be licensed, so there are no definitive lists that we could acquire. (This lack of licensing also means that the instructors aren't required to have liability insurance, although some gyms may require it if they want to be hired.)

With the two best channels unavailable, what could we do?

We created hundreds of pages of content on our website intended to rank high organically for important keywords. And we have achieved many high page-one rankings including for such topics as "Top 10 Things You Need to Know About Fitness Instructor Insurance." When people come to our site, we ask them to sign up for our newsletter, and we can use email marketing with those people. While paid search is unavailable for this, organic search activity has generated a lot of business.

These were our lead-gen maneuvers, and we budgeted for them carefully. Here's an approximation of what the math looked like on cost per lead:

CPL allowable = (CAC allowable – CPM allowable) × average lead conversion rate

CPL allowable = ($100 – $1) × 10% = $9.90

As our SEO efforts matured, we expanded toward other lead-generating strategies.

For one thing, we were able to boost our search yield via partnerships with industry leaders that also rank high, including online directories.

We used social media ads in Facebook groups as well as other communities, and we targeted people who use relevant terms to describe themselves in their social profiles on Facebook, Instagram, Reddit, TikTok, and other sites.

Visual content is important to these instructors, so Instagram was important to use for organic and paid.

Ultimately, because we spent responsibly on leads and impressions, we had the bulk of our profits left over to spend on converting leads to customers. Our allowable cost per acquisition math looked something like this:

CPA allowable = CAC allowable – (CPL allowable + CPM allowable)

CPA allowable = $100 – ($9.9 + $1) = $89.10

Despite the low CLV, this is a highly competitive space. Nonetheless, Insure Fitness has been operating profitably for several years. And we used the Lifetime Value Framework to maximize our profits.

THE BIGGEST MISTAKES IN IMPLEMENTING THE LIFETIME VALUE FRAMEWORK

There are several mistakes that I see companies make when attempting to implement the Lifetime Value Framework:

1. They have bad data. They haven't implemented the systems necessary to collect the data that CLV, CAC, CPA, CPL, etc. require. Or they have the data, but they don't have the requisite internal data analysis capabilities to make good decisions *using* that data.

2. They have internal assumptions—folklore really, or ideas that are heavily embedded in the company's culture—about why their customers buy, their loyalty, etc. And they're not open to reassessing their assumptions based on the data.

3. They aren't open to experimentation. Innovation requires an openness to experimentation and failure. You will fail. It's unavoidable if you're trying new programs. Try, succeed or fail, assess, learn, and apply your lessons. The only true failure is if you keep repeating the same mistakes. Test, test, test—forever.

4. They don't stick with the program long enough when there is a long sales cycle. Items with long sales cycles require a greater upfront investment and patience. You won't succeed if you pull the plug before you give the program a sufficient opportunity.

5. They are strictly budget-driven. They simply don't get the premise of the Lifetime Value Framework, that you shouldn't put a ceiling on your success by limiting the scale of a profitable, self-sustaining performance marketing program.

Avoid these mistakes, and you're golden. You're ready to combine the LVF with the other four tactics of SMB marketing.

That's where we're headed—toward the unification of all five tactics. Next, we'll take a look at how AI tools can help you level-up your LVF implementation. Then, we'll move on to the third tactic: understanding your customer.

AI USE CASES: LVF ENABLED BY AI

Operation
Customer Segmentation

Use AI to segment customers based on parameters such as purchase type, overall value, etc. In addition to ramping up efficiency, these tools can introduce segmentation parameters that you may not have otherwise considered, identifying trends that elude human observers.

Campaign Performance

Augment existing reporting automations. AI can combine disparate reports and study them in aggregate, generating insights that would not be visible in single-channel reporting. For example: pairing Google analytics with data on print runs and call centers may deepen your understanding of multi-channel performance.

Optimization
Financial Assessment

Put AI's superior number-crunching capabilities to work, aggregating historic data and calculating metrics discussed in this chapter, such as CLV and CAC. While this work has traditionally been done by humans, AI can dramatically reduce data entry hours, improve calculation reliability, and expand possible applications of data—including for rapid projection as well as fine-tuning by segment.

CHAPTER 3

UNDERSTANDING YOUR CUSTOMER

You don't stand a tinker's chance of producing successful
advertising unless you start by doing your homework.
—DAVID OGILVY, *Ogilvy on Advertising*[1]

In Chapter 1, we explored the first tactic of the Five-Tactic Marketing Framework: brand and performance marketing. We discovered how powerful each of those approaches is in isolation and how much more powerful they become when deployed in harmony. Then, in Chapter 2, we learned how to measure and finance those marketing efforts with the Lifetime Value Framework (tactic #2). And, at the end of each chapter, we explored how AI tools can dramatically expand and enhance our work (tactic #5). Now, it's time to tackle the missing third tactic of our framework: understanding your customer.

At the heart of any integrated marketing campaign, you'll find two questions: *whom* are we speaking to and *where* are we speaking to them?

Let's start with *whom*.

All marketing work begins with knowing your customers. We need to understand their jobs and the demands on them, what their challenges are, and what might motivate them to be interested in our products, let alone buy them.

We can't guess at this, and we certainly shouldn't assume. After all, we aren't our customers. I've successfully sold financial services, medical devices, survival supplies, consulting, and other products and services to chiropractors, yoga instructors, and outdoor enthusiasts, to name just a few. I had zero experience in those roles and industries before working on those campaigns. If I had worked from my assumptions, my personal biases, and my work experience, I would have simply been imposing my personal history, emotional motivators, and experience on a group of people who are in fact very different from me and who are motivated by different factors. This would have been a waste of time leading to an even greater waste of money.

Since we're not marketing to ourselves, we have to completely remove ourselves from the equation and look at the market objectively through observation and empathy to understand these strangers.

By the way, it goes without saying that none of what follows will matter if you don't have product–market fit. That is the essential first step and no marketing, no matter how brilliant, will save you if you don't have it. Product–market fit depends on understanding your customers, too.

HOW TO DO COMPREHENSIVE MARKET RESEARCH

Companies typically are not starting from scratch when creating new integrated, multi-channel performance campaigns. In fact, they may have years of experience selling to the market. That can be both a strength and a weakness. The strength would be the results and data produced in earlier campaigns. The potential weakness would be the fossilized assumptions that have grown up in the company, whether consciously or unconsciously, about the customers.

But what if you are starting from scratch? What if your company wants to enter a new market or put out a new product? You're basically a tourist who desires to become a landholder.

In that case, you may need to do *market research* before you embark on *customer research*.

In market research, you want to answer questions like the following:

- How large is this market?

- How fast is it growing?

- What are typical profit rates?

- Who are the major competitors?

- What are their major differentiators or advantages?

- What are people in the industry talking about?

- Why do they buy?

- What are the hidden barriers to purchasing?

- Who or what are competitors that may not be obvious?

When starting to work in a new industry, I try to come in fresh with my child's mind and practice full immersion. I'll get 18–24 months of the industry's major publication(s) and read through them. I'll read the oldest several issues from cover to cover, noting important developments, influencers, and who's advertising. Then I'll read through the rest of the issues to see how those trends are playing out and if new trends have arisen recently. The sales reps who are selling ad space in those publications may also have good insights into what's happening in the industry.

In addition to a deep dive into the industry's publications and websites, I read through major threads in online forums. The more authentic forums that you can find the better—good sources include Reddit, Facebook groups, and others.

Answers to many of these questions that I listed can be found in industry databases and analyst reports. Of course, no one database covers all industries, so you'll need to determine which databases are useful for you. If your company doesn't have access to major databases, paid researchers and analysts who do have access can produce reports for you.

And there's a cheaper way: your local library reference department may have access to business databases and be happy to help you use them, especially if they have a dedicated business library. If they don't, you could probably hire an MBA who does or a consultant via a site like Upwork, or try one of the new AI-based research tools.

It's worth noting that you may find that the databases that you consult may not necessarily agree with one another. In fact, they probably won't.[2] This takes us back to the Amazon guideline: you can't wait for perfect data that doesn't exist. Find the best data that you can and act. You can course-correct based on your own experiences as you progress.

Competitive information can be found on the internet and in other databases for free or very little money.

- The SEC's EDGAR database has free information on public companies.

- Dunn & Bradstreet has information on millions of companies.

- Hoover's MarketLine, LexisNexis, and other databases provide more information.

- LinkedIn can give you an idea of how rapidly a company is growing with the Insights information available with a premium account. This is the recent employee count insight for Salesforce.

Total employee count

Based on LinkedIn data

| 69,884 total employees | ▲ 4% 6m growth | ▲ 13% 1y growth | ▲ 31% 2y growth |

80,000				
40,000				
Aug 2020	Feb 2021	Aug 2021	Feb 2022	Aug 2022

🕒 Median tenure · 2.5 years

Pretty impressive! This will be less accurate, though, for a manufacturing or service company that has many employees who aren't on LinkedIn.

- The competitor's press releases, as well as articles written about them, will tell you what they're up to. Blog posts and social media posts from key people can be very valuable.

- Online review sites can tell you how customers perceive the strengths and weaknesses of their offerings.

- Social media listening software can give you much more insight into what's being said about a competitor and the industry in general.

You also could "secret shop" a competitor: act like a potential customer and see how they position their products and the kinds of appeals they think work.

In short, there are many ways to research the market and your competition. Dig deep—you can never know too much.

HOW TO DO COMPREHENSIVE CUSTOMER RESEARCH

When doing customer research for integrated campaigns, it's important to question all of your assumptions—which is not easy to do.

Company assumptions are often expressed as marketing personas. When I start working with a company, and they give me their marketing personas, I consider them to be source materials—the first word, not the last word. I certainly respect them and the experience and work that went into creating them, but at the same time, I will question everything about them. They have to earn their keep every day.

Assuming that the company has been in the industry for a while, the first place to look for new insights is in their customer data. Just on the surface, you can glean the following B2B factors:

- Firmographics
  - › Size of customers

> › Industry

> › Geography

> › Titles of decision-makers (and possibly influencers)

- Frequency and size of purchases

- How/where they buy

- Seasonality

- Product mix

Are there factors that distinguish the highest volume customers from lower volume ones? How do these factors differ between current customers whom you're upselling and new customers whom you close?

By reviewing the campaigns and ads that led to acquisitions and conversions in the past, you can get insights into which appeals, offers, language, and ads have been effective.

Look at the "marketing wheel" of channels. How have they used each channel—PPC, SEO, email, social media ads, blogs, groups, subreddits, affiliate/affinity partners—and what have the results been? As I mentioned in the case study in the previous chapter, sometimes the most reliable channels (like email and PPC) can be utterly ineffective for a particular market or product. Never assume!

It's important to keep in mind when reviewing historical data that this is what has worked in the past. You're looking in the rearview mirror, not through the front windshield. If the customers and market are changing—and which aren't?—you may need different appeals going forward. As the Greek philosopher Heraclitus said, "You can never step in the same river twice." This will be especially true if your goal is to expand beyond the traditional market and customers. For example, when reviewing the marketing wheel, are there channels or certain initiatives by channel that are missing? Have they been tried and been found wanting, or never tried at all?

CONTENT MARKETING

Partnerships   SEO

TV   Campaign 1   PPC

Social Media   Radio

DIRECT SELL

Partnerships   SEO

Direct Mail   Campaign 1   PPC

Social Media   Email

Much of this is quantitative data. However, some of your most important insights will be qualitative.

— *SIDEBAR* —

THREE TYPES OF DATA

In marketing, you can take advantage of three types of data.

- First-party data: First-party data is your data. It is the data that you collect from prospects and customers as they interact with your website, emails, and other materials, and when they buy from you. Since you own it, in essence, you've paid for it. Be sure to take full advantage of your very valuable first-party data.[3] It's most useful in the conversion and retention stages.

- Second-party data: Second-party data is data that you get from a partner, such as a publisher, from their sites. It's their first-party data that they're renting to you. You may, for example, use your first-party data to create a profile and then build a look-alike list and market to people using the publisher's second-party data. It's most useful in the acquisition stage.

- Third-party data: Third-party data is collected by companies like

continued

Google and Meta across many websites that they don't own. Remarketing typically relies on third-party data. Data from several third-party sources may be aggregated to create a new audience profile. Third-party data is highly regulated by laws such as the EU's GDPR and California's CCPA. As we move toward a prospective cookieless future, it will become increasingly difficult to use third-party data. It's most useful in the acquisition and conversion stages.

Developing a Qualitative Understanding of Customers

While reviewing the data, it's important to simultaneously develop a qualitative understanding of the customers that can only come from talking with them.

You need to talk directly with customers—ideally, dozens of them—to really gain insight into what drives them. You may want to visit them during the workday to see how your product is used. You can also use probing questions like these when talking with current customers in person or on the phone/Zoom:

- Can you describe the problem (that your product addresses)?

- Why did you choose to buy from us? Why did you choose not to buy from our competitors?

- How effective is our product in dealing with it? More or less than you expected?

- How could our offering be improved to make it more useful for you?

- How do you measure success?

- How much time do you spend each month on this problem? How much time did you spend before you started using our solution?

- On a scale of 1–10, how serious is this problem for you?

- How serious is this problem for your boss?

- When choosing a vendor to deal with this problem, please rank the top three factors in your decision:

  › Price

  › Quality

  › Responsiveness

  › Industry reputation

  › Innovation

  › Other

- What websites or publications do you get your industry information from? (If they say Google or X, probe more.)

- What events do you attend?

And so forth. Remember, this is a conversation. Depending on the answers you get, you need to ask probing follow-up questions. Sometimes, people who initially aren't especially forthcoming may be more so after 20 or 30 minutes of conversation. If you can provide them with an incentive to chat with you, all the better!

I also attend trade shows and interview people in the exhibition area. There's something about a person with a clipboard that makes people willing to stop and answer a few questions. And quite often, the 5 to 10 questions that you start with can lead to a 15- or 20-minute conversation that's every bit as valuable as one of those scheduled interviews. Even random attendees and speakers—or someone you meet in the elevator or buy a drink for at the bar—can give you insight into where the market is headed and what people care about. And don't forget to talk with other vendors at their booths while attendees are in their sessions.

In addition to talking with the company's current customers, you should talk to potential customers—ones who fit your ideal customer profile but aren't buying from you already. After all, they may be different. (Don't assume.) There may be reasons why some people/companies are buying from you and others aren't, even if on the surface they seem alike.

Sometimes, an established company needs an outsider, a newbie, to do these interviews. People who have been at the company for many years will simply start with too many assumptions; they won't have as open of a mind. And if customers know them, the customer may not be as forthcoming as they would be with a stranger.

As the evidence accumulates over weeks, you'll begin to see topics that resonate. It's very important to understand the emotional motivators for your customers. The specific words that people use when describing their problem and how they feel about the solution can be very important. A pro tip is to not ask them what they "think". . . Ask them how they "feel."

For many B2B buyers, their most important emotional driver is job security. In many companies, the downside to messing up is much greater than the upside to doing something very well. And employees who want to keep their jobs for a long time don't want a vendor to mess things up for them. This is especially true for large, capital-intensive purchases, as well as those working for "blue chip" brands. So, for example, being reliable—on time and on budget—and making them look good may be more important than having a breakthrough product. For a person interested in innovation, on the other hand, being the first in their industry to use a product offering a 10X improvement may be a great motivator. But for the person interested in job security and using industry-standard solutions, that may be the worst possible message.

Are your customers moving toward pleasure or away from pain? Are you selling "vitamins" or "aspirins"? What are your customers looking for?

And keep in mind this wisdom from David Ogilvy: "People don't think how they feel, they don't say what they think, and they don't do what they say."[4] People may tell you one thing but, when it comes to buying, act very differently. It's complicated!

Even the particular words that you use in your marketing can have a significant impact on your results. As we'll discuss in Chapter 6, particular words and phrases in your email subject lines, headlines, and copy can have huge impacts on your results. Some of these ("How to," "Free," "Proven") tend to work across many industries; others will be unique to your situation. You need to be listening to discover them. As my father often says—and it has been proven true time and time again—you have to put blue jeans on your words and send them off to work.

— SIDEBAR —

KNOW YOUR COFFEE!

I have a friend who was starting a B2B bulk coffee business: selling coffee to local businesses, renting them the machines, and so on.

Over drinks one night, I casually asked him how much he knew about the coffee business, to which he replied, "Nothing." I told him that I thought it was very important that he learn everything that he could quickly, given that it is a highly competitive space and coffee people are fanatical about coffee—cold brew, slow drip, the different types of beans, and so on. It's truly endless. He brushed me off saying that it was not important, that it was all about the economics.

Fast-forward three months. We were both at a happy hour at a mutual friend's house. My coffee buddy sees me walk in and immediately comes over and tells me that I could not have been more right. He had no idea how fanatical people were about coffee! He had been all but laughed out of the restaurants the first week given his lack of knowledge.

Since then, he has dedicated significant time to learning about coffee and has come to love it. He has traveled to South America

continued

and other coffee-farming continents several times. He has even become certified as a coffee sommelier.

Needless to say, his coffee business really picked up once he understood it and his customers!

Developing Personas and Segments

After doing extensive research—and the depth of research is what distinguishes outperformers—you're ready to develop personas and segments.

Personas, of course, are fictional profiles of prototypical customers. Since B2B purchases are often done by teams, your personas may include influencers and decision-makers. Typically, they'll be a few hundred words in length each and may include a representative customer photo.

For B2B, your personas will often be based on titles. You can create ideal customer profiles (ICPs) that begin with the firmographic information I listed already and then inform them with details such as the challenges they're facing, influencers, how your solution stacks up, their emotional motivators, where they get their information, and so forth. Emotional motivators may include the following:

- Why do they buy our product?

- Do they buy for need (pain) or a comparative advantage?

- What is their attitude toward our brand?

- What is their experience level?

These personas should be especially useful for the people creating content so that they better understand who they're writing for and what moves them.

— *SIDEBAR* —

A SAMPLE PERSONA

Tami Smith

Age: 47

Occupation: CFO at a prominent hospital

Role in our sale: Final approver. Mostly concerned with no increase in cost.

Information she trusts: *Wall Street Journal, Economist, Journal of Healthcare Management, Journal of Hospital Management and Health Policy*, National Center for Healthcare Leadership, peers, local and national industry associations, and conferences. Not active on professional social media; uses Instagram to connect with friends and family.

She is well aware of the cost and regulatory issues in American healthcare, as well as the competitive pressures. She's been at the same hospital for 11 years and twice in that period, it has merged with others. As the CFO, she's been central to those conversations and negotiations. She expects further consolidation in the future.

These consolidations have significantly changed her role, as some traditional CFO responsibilities have been automated or moved to the system rather than still being with the individual hospital.

At the same time, she is always thinking about controlling expenses, risk management, sources for new revenue, and better program assessments. She is very receptive to technological innovations that improve care or reduce costs. The best do both. Anything that increases costs is a non-starter.

Being a team player and being able to collaborate with others in many roles is central to her success and the success of the hospitals where she works. For us, she will trust the staff to decide as long as it doesn't increase costs.

Customer Segments

After you create personas, you can build customer segments.

Start by segmenting your current customers. Segmenting is one way around the "average" problem that I described in Chapter 2. Having different segments for your customers based on lifetime value is a great place to start. Then, you can work on moving low-value customers to the high-value segment. But that campaign will not be the campaign that you use to close new customers; that's a different segment, and they need different messages and offers.

I've worked with some companies that had fifteen or more segments or a matrix of segments: three or four age variables with gender variables with economic value variables, and so forth. Keep it simple. When you can, combine. Start with fewer segments, maybe just three or four; not more. As ABM company Demandbase writes, "When you slice your audiences that thinly, you often end up with sample sizes too small for any meaningful performance data, so decisions about what works and what doesn't may prove difficult."[5] In the future, as your program grows and becomes more sophisticated, you may be able to effectively manage more segments.

You should only consider creating a segment if it's going to affect your marketing. If men and women consider and buy your product in a similar way, don't have gender-based segments. On the other hand, Home Depot would certainly have different segments for homeowners and contractors.

Personalization

You don't need to use complex data analysis to create one-to-one marketing (unique messages and offers for each person). Your segments should be broad enough to support messaging that will appeal to everyone in them.

But you should do basic personalization. For example, when marketing to current customers, your outreach should reflect your knowledge about their previous purchases. Is there anything more annoying than a company sending you a great offer for something that you bought from them last year? On the other hand, offers for useful, complementary products are quite welcome.

You certainly can personalize your messages with the person's name (open rates are often far higher for emails that include the first name in the subject) and information. ("Since you bought X from us last year, we thought that you'd now be interested in Y.")

But beware: too much personalization can be a bad thing.

In the early 2000s, Target began using data on individual consumers to identify pregnant women—specifically those in their second trimester. The company found that they could capture these shoppers by flagging purchases of prenatal vitamins and maternity clothes. Having made a positive identification, Target would inundate the customer with coupons for things like cribs, baby clothes, and nursery furniture.[6]

This seemed like a sensible strategy, but the creepiness factor posed a real threat to Target's PR. Like when one father called Target in a fury that his teenage daughter was being inundated with mailers for pregnancy products. He didn't want a corporation encouraging his daughter to get pregnant. It was only later that he discovered the truth: his teenager really *was* pregnant. Target's analysts had figured it out before he did.

Over the years, Target learned that it had to become more savvy about its targeted advertising, revealing less about how much it knows.

Gartner put statistics to this idea in 2019, when they released a survey showing that more than half of consumers will unsubscribe from a company's communications if those communications become too personalized. And 38% will stop doing business with that company altogether.[7]

The moral of the story: when it comes to personalization, there's a difference between helpful and creepy. It's important not to lose your bearings.

Lead Scoring and ICP

Based on your company's sales history, you may be able to create an ideal customer profile (ICP). You can use this and other data for your lead scoring, too.

Once again, I've had good success by keeping lead scoring simple. A high score will look a lot like the ICP: right title, industry, company size, buying intent, etc. I do not tend to track individual pieces of content and change lead score based on the range of assets that a prospect has responded to.

However, the campaign that brought them into the funnel is very significant. For example, if a person first interacts with us through a Google search using a high-intent keyword, we will assume that they are a far more serious and immediate prospect than someone who simply downloaded a general industry ebook—hence the mention of buying intent. Rather than nurturing the first person with valuable content, we will follow up quickly with closing messages and offers.

People with abandoned shopping carts are usually in the highest value segment and certainly need immediate attention.

While marketing qualified leads (MQLs) and sales qualified leads (SQLs) may be useful for companies involved in large, enterprise sales, I haven't found them especially important in e-commerce. In e-com, lead scoring works very well.

Predictive Analytics

Frankly, traditional lead scoring as practiced by many companies is not very reliable. Scores based on pieces of content downloaded or events attended may just be a guessing game. Using the ICP only gets you a list that's basically a starting point; it's not identifying your best short-term prospects, which is what you're seeking.

If you could know your best prospects, you could target them with closing messages or, if appropriate for your industry, outreach from business development representatives (BDRs) and salespeople.

Predictive analytics or predictive lead scoring helps provide that.

Predictive analytics is based on past sales and employs machine learning. The AI software analyzes customer data in your CRM and, with some systems, supplements it with hundreds or even thousands of publicly available data points to create much more nuanced profiles of your customers. Then it scours your contacts and prospects for the ones that best match your current customers and are most likely to close within, say, the next 90 days.

Predictive lead scoring can be a very valuable addition to your performance campaigns. And that's not all that machine learning can do for you here. Stay tuned for more AI tools in a bit . . .

CASE STUDY—OUT WITH THE OLD, IN WITH THE NEW

I have a client that's been around for decades. They sell nutritional supplements to people through chiropractors. So that is B2B2C.

Their problem was that their customers—the doctors—were aging out of the market. Every year, their average customer was a year older. Although their product was still valuable, their customer base was in rapid, predictable decline. They needed new, younger physician customers.

Their performance marketing—which relied on traditional channels like direct mail, print, and phone calls—was very effective for their current customers. But it was not effective in gaining new, younger customers.

We needed to reach the younger doctors where they were. So we created a special program to do just that. We were targeting chiropractors who fell into two categories: they were in school studying or were recently licensed. Central to this was an emphasis on digital channels: paid search, organic SEO, social media, and so forth.

To reach the students, we geofenced every accredited chiropractic college in the United States (there are about 17 of them). Our digital ads would only appear to people who were frequently within a few miles of those campuses and who were looking for relevant content. We did the same with industry events.

And we had to develop content and a voice that would resonate with the younger doctors. Two topics that we focused on were the complementary nature of nutritional supplements to chiropractic care and the potential profitability of nutritional supplements for a chiropractic practice. We did half a dozen pieces of content (ebooks, infographics, and others) on each of those topics. Many of them were gated, and once people had provided us with their contact information, we could nurture them with additional pieces of content. And we then used programmatic digital ads based on remarketing, locations, and keywords.

By sponsoring faux covers and inserts, we were able to get promo materials into the school libraries via industry publications.

The new chiropractors are licensed professionals, so in most states, we could get lists of them with their contact information. This enabled email marketing. And once they were licensed, they were in the same professional online communities as older chiropractors, so we could reach both through those.

This multi-channel program meant that between their student years and their new doc years, these individuals would see my client's messages for five or six years. In just the first three years of our program, we had over two million highly targeted impressions and generated many leads in a cost-effective manner.

We understood the customer, and our segmentation of them was very successful.

The Multi-Dimensional Customer

If there's one thing you take away from this chapter, I hope it'll be this: that your customers are multi-dimensional people, and that, as a marketer, it's your job to understand and account for all of that dimension. That's what everything in this chapter has been building toward. We study markets, build personas, parse out segments, and pursue personalization all with that same end in mind: to understand and speak to the full dimensionality of our customers.

But before we unify the five tactics of SMB marketing, we must dive into integrated campaigns. At the top of this chapter, I said that multi-channel strategy addresses two key questions: *whom* are we speaking to and *where* are we speaking to them. In the next chapter, we'll tackle that latter question, rounding out our understanding of integrated campaigns.

First though, let's take a quick look at how AI tools can expand and enhance what we know about our customers.

AI USE CASES:
CUSTOMER UNDERSTANDING ENABLED BY AI

Creation
Market Research

Use generative AI to simulate the experience of sitting across the table from experts in any given market. These AIs are great at aggregating information and summarizing findings. Learn about key spheres of influence, market trends, and target habits. Distill large collections of text for a quick study of your target. Example: If selling insurance to newly graduated physical therapists, feed a PT textbook into your AI and get back a high-level summary. Insights into your target's education may reveal new opportunities for connecting and adding value.

Expert Source Identification

If that AI-powered research leaves you hungry for human insight, ask the AI to identify potential partners for knowledge sharing and/or collaboration. The AI will recommend experts in the market, as well as key knowledge bases and major influencers.

Customer Persona Creation

Rapidly create customer personas from scratch with AI or build them based on existing data. If you don't already have a feel for what your personas should look like, the AI can study your inputs and recommend a few possible customer bases, with persona briefs for each. If you already know what the persona should look like, give the AI your top-level insights, and it will write a brief in response.

Targeted Content Generation

Various neural network types (including transformers and recurrent neural networks) empower AIs to create new content that's inspired by old content. This means that you can input content that's already proven successful in your market, and the AI will output new content with a similar contour.

Operation

Segmentation

For automated segmentation, simply give the AI a first-party, second-party, or third-party database of leads, prospects, and/or customers. The AI will analyze your data, recommend segmentation strategies, and implement them as needed. You can give it segmentation parameters, or let the AI select those parameters on its own.

CHAPTER 4

THE NEED FOR INTEGRATED CAMPAIGNS AND MULTI-CHANNEL EXECUTION

*Everyone has a plan until
they get punched in the mouth.*

—MIKE TYSON[1]

Plans are worthless, but planning is everything.
—GENERAL DWIGHT EISENHOWER[2]

We're nearly ready to put our Five-Tactic Marketing Framework into action. We've tackled brand and performance marketing, we continue to look at AI use cases, and we have discussed the Lifetime Value Framework and the importance of understanding your customer. But we haven't yet addressed the essence of integrated campaigns and multi-channel strategy. That's what we'll be doing here, in Chapter 4.

Integrated campaigns are a specific subtype of marketing concerned with deploying a unified message across many channels (also called "multi-channel marketing"). Unfortunately, it's become fashionable to study and implement integrated campaigns as a single, one-stop solution for all SMB marketing woes. But just as neither brand nor performance marketing alone can really skyrocket a company, integrated campaigns have a limited impact when operationalized unilaterally. And integrated campaigns will not work without understanding your customer.

But before we can unify the five tactics, we need to establish a deep understanding of integrated campaigns and the unique insights that multi-channel thinking brings to our work. That's what we'll tackle in this chapter and the one that follows.

You see, managing just one campaign in one marketing channel can be challenging for some small and midsize businesses (SMBs), especially when they're first ramping up their marketing programs. But to be truly effective, you need a multi-channel marketing program.

A multi-channel program may simultaneously run across email, paid search, organic search, paid social, organic social, industry sites, remarketing, print, direct mail, webinars, TV, radio, podcasts, and other channels. It's not easy to launch and manage, but it is critical for optimizing your returns with the Five-Tactic Marketing Framework.

Why?

For many reasons.

First, not everyone in your market is hanging out in the same place. If you want to reach your entire target market—as you should—you need to be everywhere, or at least in a lot of places. And for those people who are active in many places, seeing your messages and offers repeatedly increases their impact and odds for success. Your conversion rates will be significantly higher than if you only use one channel. Properly executed, the different channels "lift" one another—the whole is greater than the sum of the parts.

Different people learn and absorb information in different ways. Some respond to text, some to images, some to video, and so forth. For example, video is especially good for communicating emotional messages, which is why major companies spend tens of billions of dollars on TV ads annually.

By taking advantage of multiple channels, you can provide a range of messages and content that are more likely to engage your full market. One set of researchers wrote, "Over the last decade, advertisers increasingly and successfully have used multi-platform communications to achieve synergistic results in getting messages across to consumers within a single marketing campaign."[3] These results are typical.

Remember: 43% of B2B buyers prefer a representative-free buying experience, and it's even higher among Millennials,[4] so you need to get in the target customer's face for them to notice and buy from you.

Some retailers have found that "omnichannel customers spend two to five times more than customers who buy in only one channel."[5]

Marketing in one channel actually lifts results in other channels where you're not marketing. For example, "online advertising has been found to have significant effects on offline sales."[6]

B2B studies are harder to do than B2C because the buying teams have so many members and the sales cycles are typically much longer. But the impact of multi-channel is as great or even greater in B2B for companies that use it to stay in front of all the members of the buying team over months.

Even if your customer is not ready to buy, and most won't be, your multi-channel campaign will help build mental availability so that you are top of mind when they are.

And just the fact that you are marketing increases trust in your company: you must be a real player and be planning to be around for a long time if you're spending on marketing.

On the other hand, if a potential customer hears of you and starts to do research and just finds an ugly, old website or an abandoned Facebook page, that is not likely to earn their trust. In fact, it will hurt your chances to win their business.

Note: although you probably have gathered this by now, when I talk about multi-channel marketing, I'm not talking about sales and distribution channels like retail, resellers, partners, etc. This is about marketing communication channels.

— *SIDEBAR* —

ESTABLISH YOUR NORTH STAR

You'll be undertaking multi-channel campaigns that certainly will last many months and, in most cases, will last years. You need to firmly establish your program goals at the beginning so you can refer to them and use them to benchmark your results.

Your goals may be to raise awareness, acquire new leads, close new customers, upsell existing customer accounts, or something else. You need to have the goals and how you will measure against them agreed on in writing before the launch of the campaign.

The goals must be measurable. If you're raising awareness, how many impressions do you need? If it's leads or sales or upsells, how many? Be very specific in defining success. Note: for new teams and campaigns, you may want to start with channels that aren't impression-based so you can build confidence for yourself and the execs with more material, revenue-oriented results.

Then, report on how well you're doing at achieving those goals—and not some different or new goals that someone might bring up after the program has launched but that the program was never designed to achieve.

More marketing campaigns fail and more marketing teams lose their funding because they did not get a consensus with leadership on what constitutes success BEFORE the launch of their efforts.

THE IMPORTANCE OF CHANNEL SELECTION

In general, success in multi-channel performance marketing is based on the following:

- Targeting 40%—the target or list of a specific audience

- Offers 40%—the reason they should act

- Creative, etc. 20%

So, effective targeting is essential to success. And largely, you target first through your channel selection and then the available channel-specific targeting parameters.

Multi-channel marketing is not random. It's not just a matter of throwing things at the wall and seeing what sticks. You need to start with a multi-channel plan that is tailored to your audience and then modify it based on the results you achieve. (Note: this multi-channel plan is also often called your "media mix.")

Remember that you're not marketing to yourself. Don't assume that your customers are where you are. Fifty-two percent of marketers are on X (formerly "Twitter"),[7] but only 23% of the general public in the United States is.[8]

You want to start with the insights that you gained from the customer research you did (as described in the previous chapter). Some factors to consider are the following:

- Are the customers a digitally savvy group? If so, which social media sites do they use? Which online communities? (Facebook? LinkedIn? Instagram? Reddit? TikTok? Discord? Industry-specific sites?)

- What industry sites and publications did they tell you they used? What events? Keep in mind that these give you access to a premium audience and often have corresponding extraordinarily high rates.

- Do you have or can you get a good email list? Usually, email lists only perform well if people have opted in to them, so the company's legacy list may be useful. However, you may be able to use an acquired or purchased list for targeting social media and programmatic ads. Or use the acquired list for emails that promote a *very* high-value piece of content that may get people to opt in.

- For paid search, you can do keyword research (that is also useful for organic) and determine if paid ads might be cost-effective. Tools like SpyFu and SEMrush give you a good idea of the top keywords and ads of your competitors. Remember that some keywords suggest very high purchase intent and others are for more general industry interest. You'll want to use them differently.

- For organic search, look at the companies that dominate the search engine results pages (SERPs) now—remembering that over half of organic clicks are on the top three page-one results.[9] Are they industry leaders so entrenched that it would take you a long time to replace them? Or do you have a shot at high rankings in a few months?

- Could you use programmatic ad platforms like Propellant and AdRoll that enable you to target like the big guys, using email lists, third-party site remarketing, search retargeting, and other approaches?

- Is seasonality a major factor? For example, turkeys are mostly sold at Thanksgiving, chocolate and roses fly off the shelves in February, and gym memberships are bought most often at the beginning of the year.

You'll want to build a multi-channel program with typically four to six channels for peak effectiveness. Some channels will be more efficient than others. Start with the channels that are speediest and that you expect will be the most cost-effective and then add in the next most efficient ones.[10]

In general, paid channels will perform faster, but in the long run, organic may perform better. You may want a two-track strategy to emphasize paid channels in the short run but build organic for the long term. This is very similar to the distinction between brand-based and performance-based advertising we discussed in Chapter 1.

While I wish I could provide you with a worksheet to figure out how to allocate your budget between channels, it is largely a matter of experience. Some companies and agencies use media planners whose entire job is to study and recommend the best media mix and budget allocation.

— SIDEBAR —

DIFFERENT STROKES FOR DIFFERENT FOLKS

As I mentioned in the case studies in the previous two chapters, not every channel is for everyone or every campaign. With the young chiropractors, email and paid search weren't available, while traditional channels like direct mail had been effective with the older docs. Competitors had priced paid search out of the market for the fitness instructors. But in both these and other cases, effective alternatives were available.

Different channels may be more or less effective depending on your objectives. For example, email may be especially effective for customer retention and growth campaigns since the messages will be coming from a known and trusted source. Your current customers may also be open to coming to an event.

For a few years, marketers have claimed that direct mail is making a comeback.[11] One reason is that it has far less competition in the mailbox. Mail has dropped by over 33%, so a direct mail piece may now stand out. Traditionally, direct mail has been especially effective with seniors. Will it work with your B2B customers? Attractive three-dimensional mailers can really get your prospect's attention and be effective. But if you're marketing to 500,000 businesses, start with a small test.

continued

Video is typically effective for brand campaigns that build mental availability.

Paid search is typically effective for acquisition stage campaigns. People using keywords with high intent should be taken straight to conversion landing pages.

Social media and digital display ads can be effective for content offers, which you can use to build your list, too.

You need to carry your branding and your campaign themes across all these channels to have the multi-channel impact you're paying for. The biggest mistake that many companies make is not branding their creative; this greatly reduces the likelihood that people will remember them when they need to buy their type of offering. The second biggest mistake they make is they don't have a clear call to action on all their creative. Amazing as it may seem, just adding a "Learn More" button to a digital display ad can improve your click-through rate (CTR) by 10X.

Consider your audience, your objectives, and which channel will work best for you.

LAUNCHING YOUR CAMPAIGNS

Now comes the fun part: developing your creative and launching and optimizing your multi-channel performance marketing campaigns.

To do this, you must tie your media plan to your funnel stages. For example, working from the bottom up, email may be your most important channel for increasing lifetime value with current customers. You can supplement it with programmatic ads and other channels. For your conversion and acquisition stages, other channels may play a more important role. Of course, you may use some channels in all stages, but your targeting, creative, offers, and so forth will vary by funnel stage.

After you've run your campaigns for a few weeks, you may have enough data to begin to optimize them. Don't do this too early on insufficient data!

If a channel is underperforming, is it because your audience mostly isn't on that channel? Some offers are performing well, but others aren't? Some creative is doing great, but other creative is falling flat?

For a paid search campaign, you may want to perform A/B tests. Consider the following:

- What are you measuring? Clicks usually aren't enough. Are you looking for people to provide contact information? To download something? To buy?

- When you set up your ads in AdWords, specify that Google shouldn't optimize your campaigns. You want random rotation, even though Google will tell you that that won't produce optimal results.

- The larger your sample size, the lower your margin of error. And you'll need a much larger sample size to achieve statistically significant results if you're selling to 5,000 people rather than 50,000.

- After you've collected sufficient data, you can analyze with your A/B test calculator. You want to achieve a 90% confidence interval.

On the surface, this is straightforward enough, but in practice, it can be challenging. The ad with the highest clickthrough rate may not lead to the most purchases. The "losing" ad or offer may, in fact, simply be appealing to a different part of your audience. You may be better off if you use both.

You may find that some channels are doing great, and you could temporarily cut back your investment in those and still reach your goals and put the funds into other channels that aren't hitting their mark yet. Don't "optimize" by only retaining your top-performing channels and creative or, pretty soon, you won't have a multi-channel campaign; you'll have a single-channel campaign that'll soon be exhausted.

And when you find that your creative is getting exhausted, be ready to refresh it with new creative, using the previous winners as your control. This is extremely important—just because you are bored with the creative does not mean that it is not still effective with your target audience. Be sure to test new concepts against those with proven performance. Only then will you know if it is time for a wholesale change.

You can only go so far in optimizing some channels. You're limited, of course, by how many of your contacts are in that channel and what tools are available to you. There will only be so many searches on particular keywords in Google search each month, and there's nothing you can do to increase that. And usually, you should not aspire to 100% impression share: the cost per click (CPC) will start rising sharply when you exceed 80% impression share, so unless your target customer acquisition cost can justify the higher CPC, stop while you are profitable.

It will be the rare trial that completely bombs or goes through the roof immediately. At a minimum, expect to run programs for six months for a reasonable trial.

And avoid what analytics maven Avinash Kaushik calls "data puking": looking at a lot of data with no point, no story behind it.[12] Do email opens matter if they don't correlate to leads and sales? Your review of data will not just produce short-term insights but should also, over time, give you a much more nuanced understanding of your customers.

Finally, be sure that your marketing is always on. Turning it on and off seriously undermines its effectiveness:

> [Byron Sharp] advised marketers aiming for reach and frequency balance to divide their annual budget into 50 weekly portions, or "every month [spend] about a twelfth taking account for seasonality". Advertisers should "never bunch exposures" and should stop thinking about "bursts" of advertising, "because bursting means going silent at other times", added Sharp.[13]

A story often told in the marketing world about Professor Philip Kotler was that he was once flying in a commercial airplane with a student seated next to him. The student questioned how important advertising really is—what would happen to a company if they just stopped advertising altogether? Kotler replied that to stop advertising would be similar to losing the engines on the plane: at first, the change would be very little, but eventually, it would crash into the ground.

If you have budget concerns or constraints, consider dialing back marketing spend to a point of comfort, but do not turn it all the way off. Some exposure in the market will keep you relevant and let potential consumers know you are still in business. A sudden departure from market presence can have an extremely adverse effect on both current and prospective customers.

— *SIDEBAR* —

CREATING A GREAT CROSS-CHANNEL CUSTOMER EXPERIENCE

When possible, create a great cross-channel customer experience. Customers should be recognized as at the same point in the relationship or transaction on all channels, regardless of how they interact with you. For example, an abandoned shopping cart campaign should be aware of the contents of the shopping cart, the offer made and terms, and whether the person views it on desktop or mobile.

Consulting firm McKinsey says that "customer experience is king."[14] B2C companies have typically provided much better customer experiences than B2B companies, but the best B2B companies are gaining a competitive edge by consumerizing their experiences and providing what people want.

continued

> Steve [Jobs] embraced the marketing adage that every single moment a consumer encounters a brand—whether as a buyer, a user, a store visitor, a passerby seeing a billboard, or someone simply watching an ad on TV—is an experience that adds either credits or debits to the brand's 'account' in his imagination. The 'Apple experience' was an unprecedented merger of marketing and technology excellence that made customers want to come back for more.[15]

As noted before, creating and managing successful multi-channel campaigns is complicated and requires experience. Similarly, you may need to build new internal skills to create a great cross-channel customer experience.

In a related matter, there is an active discussion in marketing about how much customers care about the "why" of a company: its purpose. Some, like Simon Sinek, say that it is very important. Others say that customers rarely know or care about a company's "Why" and are only concerned about WIIFM: What's In It For Me. No doubt it varies from company to company and even customer to customer.

Patagonia certainly profits from its strong connection to the outdoors community, as reflected in the opening paragraph of its core values:

> Our criteria for the best product rests on function, repairability, and, foremost, durability. Among the most direct ways we can limit ecological impacts is with goods that last for generations or can be recycled so the materials in them remain in use. Making the best product matters for saving the planet.[16]

Outstanding customer support, reflected in how well it stands behind its products, is central to its success, too.

> We guarantee everything we make. If you are not satisfied with one of our products at the time you receive it, or if one

of our products does not perform to your satisfaction, return it to the store you bought it from or to Patagonia for a repair, replacement or refund. Damage due to wear and tear will be repaired at a reasonable charge.[17]

They don't just talk the talk, they walk the walk, and that translates their Why into an outstanding customer experience.

HUBSPOT AND THE LIMITS OF INBOUND-ONLY

We have talked about HubSpot before, and it is a great example of a phenomenally successful company. Founded in Cambridge, MA, in 2006, today it has over 150,000 customers in more than 120 countries and a market cap of over $14 billion.[18]

HubSpot went to market with marketing software, but it had the genius to not sell the software but the benefit. Central to this was branding and proselytizing the "inbound marketing" approach. Instead of selling what has traditionally been complicated software to do something that many SMBs don't want to do (marketing), they were selling an approach and an enabling tool for something that SMBs really do want to do: generate more leads and sales.

Inbound marketing, of course, is the idea that you should produce a lot of valuable and entertaining content (blog posts, ebooks, videos, etc.), distribute them via organic social posts, and get high search rankings so that qualified people will find them and you when they are looking for what you're selling. The theory is that, in the long run, this will be more effective than interrupting customers with ads, cold calls, bulk emails, etc. ("outbound marketing") when they're actually interested in other things.

Inbound marketing made a lot of sense in 2006. The internet only had about 85 million websites; today it has over 1.1 billion.[19] Perhaps most importantly, search rankings were not nailed down then. They were much more fluid. With effort (with very little effort in some industries) you could quickly get high rankings.

Today, it's a very different world. As SEO maven Rand Fishkin wrote in 2018, one of the ignored truths of SEO is "less opportunities for small sites and emerging companies as a few big players dominate an ever-increasing share of Google's top results."[20] This has only gotten worse since then.

How did inbound marketing work for early HubSpot? According to a 2009 *Harvard Business School* case study, after three years, they had 1,000 customers.[21] Pretty good start! But inbound was highly inefficient: their website was seeing about 100,000 visitors a month, and they were generating about 1,000 leads a month, but they were only closing about 35 new deals.

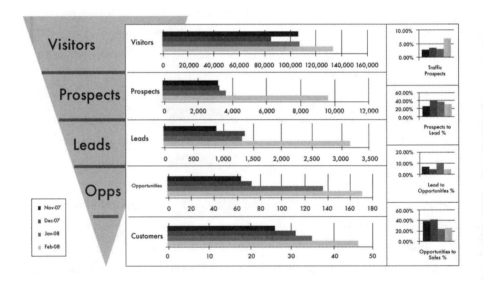

And they were spending millions of dollars on inbound. By May 2008, they had raised $17.5 million from VCs (they would raise $100.5 million before going public in 2014).[22] They would ultimately be publishing over 1,000 new pieces of content a year.

Did the efficiency of their inbound marketing improve as they scaled their spend from millions to tens of millions? No. Based on the publicly available data that they provided as part of their S1 and first 10-K annual report, Louis Gudema reported that from 2011 to 2014 their customer acquisition cost (CAC) increased from $6,671 per new customer to $11,997—a 79.8% increase in just four years.[23] And this was after doing inbound for eight years. OMG.

What was the problem? One problem is that when you toss a very wide net, a lot of the fish that wander in aren't remotely qualified or close to buying. In their 2014 "Year in Review," HubSpot reported that their top five most-read blog posts were the following:

1. How to Set Gmail as Your Browser's Default Email Client

2. What No One Tells You About Your Career When You're 22

3. 9 Hilarious Out-of-Office Email Auto-Replies

4. The Best Cold Email Pitch I've Ever Gotten

5. The 7 Elements of Modern Web Design[24]

Except perhaps for number four, those aren't likely to be attracting highly qualified decision-makers for buying marketing software.

In competitive content markets, you may need a lot of content—over 100 blog posts, for example—to begin to move the needle, as this chart from HubSpot illustrates.

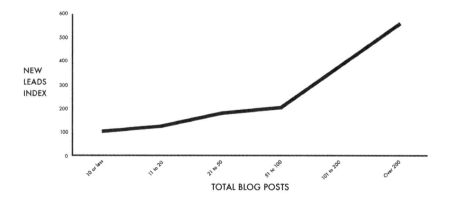

IMPACT OF TOTAL PUBLISHED BLOG POSTS ON INBOUND LEADS

How many SMBs will do that and wait that long?

This isn't unusual. Mature B2B enterprise inbound programs often need 300–400 new contacts to generate one new customer, which is why many B2B companies have adopted account-based marketing (ABM) for bigger accounts.

My break-even-then-profit model for applying the Lifetime Value Framework does not anticipate losing tens of millions of VC dollars before achieving profitability.

I advocate the use of a full, multi-channel approach. Highly targeted programmatic and social media ad tools that didn't exist in 2006 are highly effective, as is remarketing. Partnerships are often highly efficient. For the right situation, we'll use direct mail, then events, and even telesales as a last resort.

Don't be guided by a philosophy. Think critically and figure out which combination of channels is likely to work best for your situation. And then test, test, test.

As I said before, use paid advertising for speed and organic for the long run. And for the best results, use them both.

PERFORMANCE MARKETING HALF-LIFE

In traditional performance marketing, campaign half-life is a way to figure out when you have gotten roughly half the deals that you are likely to get from that campaign.

Half-life is based on the long-tail concept—the same one we saw in Chapter 2 when we were looking at high-order-value buyers and lower-order-value buyers. In fact, the two concepts are so similar that we can use the same graph to illustrate both.

In this case, the graph illustrates that you're likely to get most of your deals pretty quickly, with a longer tail over several weeks or months. When you've reached the halfway point, you know that you can judge the efficacy of the campaign without waiting for the rest of the results. You base the calculation on historical data, which will vary for each market. Digital marketing tools offer so much data and analytics that it can be easy to figure out.

Email half-life is typically very short. Most of your opens and clicks will happen in the first couple of hours after the email is sent.

The half-life for a particular offer or piece of content may be much longer, months even. Most will become exhausted at some point, and you'll need new efforts or new offers.

Occasionally, you will create an evergreen, an offer that just keeps performing, and you can use it to continue to appeal to "Ogilvy's Parade" (that steady stream of new people coming into the market every year). We're all in search of the Aflac duck or Progressive Flo that continues to perform for years.

You need to always be testing against your control, but until something new beats it, it's the champion, and you need to keep running it until it's not, no matter how bored you personally may be with it.

CASE STUDY—
KICKING ASANAS AND TAKING NAMASTES

In 2014, we wanted to start another brand. So, as we always do, we researched many markets. Three of the most important criteria we consider for going forward are the following:

- Total addressable market (TAM) has to be large enough to support significant, profitable growth.

- Keyword research shows an active online community that can be reached through inexpensive and automated digital channels.

- Top search keywords are not so competitive that they've been priced out of reach (although, in Chapter 2, I went over a case where paid search was too expensive, but we were successful anyway using other channels).

We did our usual, very in-depth customer research. I personally spoke with over 30 yoga instructors. What jumped out to me was that, while these were typically solopreneurs, they did not really think like businesspeople. They were motivated by the health, spiritual, and aesthetic aspects of yoga, not its potential for income or revenue growth. The average instructor nationwide only makes about $30,000 annually. A few superstars take home six-figure incomes. They do care about the Why of their vendors. Insurance was not high on their minds.

This is very different from how I think. So if we went into this market, I could not make marketing for myself. I would have to put myself into their shoes and their frame of mind to be successful.

Many of the instructors might not buy the insurance of their own volition but because a school that they are teaching at requires them to have it. Our mobile website would have to be very good because, literally, a person might buy the insurance in their car just before going inside to teach their first class.

We decided to create beYogi to sell insurance to yoga instructors with additional benefits for our members, the people who bought their insurance through us.[25] Yoga instructors have a unique personality that distinguishes them from other solopreneurs, and so the integrated, multi-channel strategy had to be specifically tailored to them.

Once again, we were working with a very low maximum customer acquisition cost—just $79. That meant that direct mail was out, and telesales was used only rarely to close the deal when it appeared that the person was ready to buy. But we ramped up a program using virtually all digital channels, partnerships, and events. The following is an example of a banner ad that was quite effective for us.

As discussed before, email is great for renewals, nurturing leads, and upselling existing customers but not so valuable for closing new customers. You don't need to be licensed to be a yoga instructor, so state lists are not available. We tried buying, renting, and compiling lists that supposedly were yoga professionals, but lists that people haven't opted into usually aren't effective for email marketing. Those lists were somewhat useful for targeting social media ads and programmatic advertising, but they still weren't very effective: the qualifications for being on these lists simply weren't tight enough.

Paid search was useful, especially for people looking to buy a policy *now*, and for building a home-grown email list that we could then nurture with further information and offers. We ungated some content but gated the most valuable content.

Our content had two main tracks. We have content and offers focused on closing the deal for high-intent people, like those searching on "best yoga instructor insurance" or "yoga instructor liability insurance."

And then we have top-of-funnel content for people who are looking for information on being a yoga instructor. Some popular items are the following:

- The Ultimate Guide for Yoga Instruction for Men

- An ebook on helping your students align their chakras

- The ultimate 2022 yoga class playlist

We were pleasantly surprised when "The Badass Guide to Yoga for Men" crushed it.

Home › Yoga Styles & Methods › Basics › **The Badass Guide to Yoga for Men**

The Badass Guide to Yoga for Men

Published by 👤 Tristan Gatto at 🕐 May 27, 2016   Tags ▾   Categories ▾

I know what you're thinking: another article about why more men should do yoga.

But listen up, guys, because it's time to get real. Below are seven hardcore facts to support incorporating a solid yoga practice into your life as well as six badass yoga poses for men. After all, one man's loss is another man's gain—and it's time for more gains, bruh.

SEO has been very valuable. Over time, we've grown our site to over 1,000 pages. We now have thousands of backlinks. While we focus our efforts on less than 100 very important keywords for paid and organic, as I write this, according to SpyFu, we get traffic from over 29,000 keywords—over 2,500 listed on page one of Google's SERPs—up from 15,900 keywords a year ago. This produces approximately 17,500 clicks a month, which otherwise would cost us over $30,000 per month to generate, if we even could. SEO is the gift that keeps giving.

Of course, we've had surprises along the way. The tagline "Kicking Asanas and Taking Namastes" took off in a big way. Later, when we created a library of yoga poses, one pleasant surprise was how much traffic we generated by just adding the Sanskrit names of the poses to the page. People using the Sanskrit names were much more advanced in their yoga career too.

Yoga Pose Library

Our Yoga Pose Library includes hundreds of poses for each level from beginner through advanced, for different areas of the body, and also by type of pose. This allows yoga practitioners to find the perfect pose for an individual needs. From Awkward Pose to Wild Thing, yogis of all levels can benefit from learning proper form. Even with careful instruction, many liabilities exist for yoga instructors making Yoga Liability Insurance extremely important to have.

Baby Cobra Pose
(Bhujanga)

Awkward Pose
(Utkatasana)

Bound Angle Pose
(Baddha Konasana)

Bharadvaja's Twist
(Bharadvajasana)

Boat Pose
(Paripurna Navasana)

Camel Pose
(Ustrasana)

Bow Pose
(Dhanurasana)

I talk about conversion tactics more in a later chapter, but with beYogi, we have two types of offers and landing pages. For clicks from paid ads like search, where we're looking for an immediate payoff in the form of contact information (at the very least), we use landing pages with a prominent call to action and form at the top. Those "dead" pages also don't have any site navigation: the only thing that you can do on them is use the form. However, we do have other pages on the site in which the content itself is of value and the CTA, the offer, is lower value, and the form may be embedded halfway down the page.

Once people sign up for any offer, they receive a welcoming email, at the very least. Depending on whether they are now a prospect or a customer, the email content that they get going forward will be different.

We measure intent by what type of campaign they came to us from and how much they are engaging with, as well as the type of content. For high-intent prospects, the communications are very aggressive, pushing specific benefits and endorsements from current members to induce them to buy now.

An abandoned shopping cart gets, of course, the highest intent rating. At the minimum it gets emails; it may even get a phone call if we have their number.

Partnerships with professional associations are successful. We offer a discount for their members, or a revenue share with the organization, or a combination of the two. Professional associations typically provide good platforms for ads, too.

Some yoga chains require instructors to carry their own insurance, so we partner with them as well.

Social media is huge for this community. They are concerned with aesthetics, the technique of the pose, and yoga's philosophical nature. So, while for tax accountants you might want long-form technical pieces, for the yoga community, image-based media are very effective. Instagram is huge; Facebook is also effective for older members. Video is so-so, making TikTok a decent channel as well.

For events, we don't go to consumer-focused yoga events like Sat Nam Fest that have thousands of people attending. We go to instructor-focused events that just 100–200 professionals attend.

Once someone buys a policy from beYogi, they are a member, and they get a higher tier of content, additional offers like discounts from Gaiam, and business forms and waivers (what I think of as a business in a box), so the relationship is continuous and value-added.

In 2022, the beYogi website averaged about 25,000 new visitors a month with about 5% of them turning into new customers. That's at least an order of magnitude better than the HubSpot numbers that I mentioned earlier. That's the difference between profit and loss.

Our goal was to be operating profitably after six months—we made it in four. After three years, beYogi was the leading provider of insurance for yoga instructors. Today, we are profitably adding tens of thousands of new members annually with an opportunity still for 10X growth.

FIVE-TACTIC MARKETING, HERE WE COME

Together, this chapter and the one that preceded it have given us a complete overview of integrated campaigns, helping us to identify both *whom* we're speaking to and *where* we're speaking to them.

All told, the first part of this book has tackled each of the tactics in our Five-Tactic Marketing Framework: brand and performance marketing (tactic #1), the Lifetime Value Framework (tactic #2), understanding your customer (tactic #3), integrated campaigns (tactic #4), and AI tools (tactic #5).

Now it's time for us to put the Framework into action, exploring how it rolls out across the entire funnel—from impressions through post-conversion. That will be the focus of Part II, where we'll tackle each level of the funnel, one by one, discovering again and again that true marketing power comes not from any one tactic alone, but from the unification and application of all five tactics, in strategic harmony.

But first, of course, a look at the fifth tactic, where we'll see how you can use AI tools to expand and enhance your multi-channel integrated campaign efforts . . .

AI USE CASES: MULTI-CHANNEL EXECUTION ENABLED BY AI

Creation

Campaign Material Creation

As we've seen before, generative AI can be an excellent tool for ideating, writing, and graphic designing. These applications become especially useful in multi-channel contexts: we need a large volume of campaign materials, often with very specific parameters around word count and image dimensions. Generative AIs can follow prescribed parameters, creating this additional volume in virtually no time at all, and at no additional cost.

Marketing Mix Modeling

Your AI can model various campaigns and/or select the most effective channel mix based on market research. Being computational wizzes, AIs can consider innumerable channel mix permutations and measure those options against your context and objectives.

Integrated Campaign Project Planning

Once you have an idea of what the campaign will look like, ask your AI to create materials lists, rollout schedules, and other action plans necessary to ensure proper execution.

Operation
Attribution Modeling

As we discussed in Chapter 1, attribution modeling represents one of the most challenging sub-fields of performance marketing—and one of the greatest opportunities for implementing AI. That capability becomes most important when deploying multi-channel campaigns, where it's often difficult to determine which channel is responsible for delivering the lion's share of results. Here, we can use AI tools to test different models, run those models against one another, and determine which performs best (using a neural networking process called "backpropagation"). From there, you can use the AI's insights to optimize your spend and attention across channels.

PART II

Applying the Five-Tactic Marketing Framework

Welcome to Part II, where we'll explore how the Five-Tactic Marketing Framework operates in practice. In the next three chapters, we'll tackle each stage of the marketing funnel, discovering precisely how a unified deployment of all five tactics works—as well as why each tactic is vital to our efforts.

That effort begins in Chapter 5, with the acquisition stage, which brings together . . .

- Brand-based impressions and lead-generating performance marketing (tactic #1)

- Spending metrics powered by the Lifetime Value Framework (tactic #2)

- Deep knowledge of the target customer (tactic #3)

- Integrated-campaign insights surrounding customer targeting and multi-channel deployment (tactic #4)

- AI tools that expand and enhance our acquisition efforts across all tactics (tactic #5)

By the end of Part II, we will have discovered how high performers unite marketing tactics to break plateaus and deliver profits.

ENJOYING THE BOOK?
PLEASE LEAVE A REVIEW!

If you've found *Outmarket the Competition* helpful, I would greatly appreciate it if you could take a moment to leave a review on Amazon.

Your feedback helps other readers discover the book and supports me in continuing to provide valuable content.

Just scan the QR code below to leave your review.

FAST COMPANY *Press*

TOOLS AND RESOURCES

Tools and resources are constantly evolving. To stay ahead of the curve and ensure you're leveraging the latest advancements, it's crucial to have the newest tools at hand.

That's why I've created a dedicated section on my website where you can access a curated list of the most current and effective tools and resources by category.

Simply scan the QR code below to explore:

Link address: https://nickdoyle.com/resources

FAST
COMPANY
Press

CHAPTER 5

ACQUISITION

*I have seen one advertisement actually sell not twice as much,
not three times as much, but 19½ times as much as another.
Both advertisements occupied the same space. Both were run
in the same publication. Both had photographic illustrations.
Both had carefully written copy. The difference was that one
used the right appeal and the other used the wrong appeal.*

—JOHN CAPLES (cited by Ogilvy)[1]

Arguably, acquisition is the funnel stage where the five-tactic approach matters most. And that's in large part because of the funnel's width here. The top of the funnel is wide—far wider than you'll see in any illustration. It contains your total addressable market. That may be people at a few hundred businesses, a few thousand, or even tens or hundreds of thousands.

Acquisition is a challenging stage because you may be pursuing three very important but distinct goals simultaneously. The reason for this is that you are targeting prospects with different levels of buying intent:

1. Little to no buying intent: These people are at industry events or interested in industry content but are not ready to commit to giving you any information. Build awareness and mental availability for your brand by establishing expertise and adding value, which will produce long-term results.

2. **Limited buying intent:** These people are actively searching for specific information. Generate leads by getting people to provide their contact information in exchange, typically, for expertise such as an industry study or ebook.

3. **High buying intent:** These people are showing buying indicators—actively scheduling demos, searching with purchase intent, etc. Close the sale by enticing people to go straight to the purchase.

The key Lifetime Value Framework metrics in this stage are cost per thousand impressions (CPM) and cost per lead (CPL).

In the acquisition stage, you make your first impression (we all know how important that is) and ask contacts to start engaging with you. A few will go straight to buying, but most will first engage with your content in whichever of the many forms they encounter it.

In the first subset mentioned—buyers with little to no intent—you may just be looking to increase the target's awareness of your company, and you'll be running first-tactic campaigns solely designed to generate impressions and build your company's mental availability. You won't be shooting for clicks or sign-ups. This is totally legitimate, and this brand building will make your campaigns with CTAs more effective. That's what we saw in Chapter 1: utilizing brand and performance marketing to complement one another.

If your marketing program is well established and has the confidence of the senior team, you have the option to run these brand-building campaigns. But if you're just starting out and need to build their confidence, I would recommend that you not run campaigns whose success is solely measured on the number of impressions produced. Undoubtedly, you'll be asked, "We spent X dollars. What was the return?" and you won't have a satisfactory answer. Start out with programs with more measurable results that everyone can get and stay behind.

To get a customer to raise their hand and become a lead, you need to create superior offers and a better user experience using the knowledge about them that you gathered in your considerable integrated-campaign research. Assuming you're targeting your messages well, a great offer can perform many times better than a poor one (or, more accurately, infinitely better since a poor offer won't produce any results).

In the acquisition stage, your messaging and content will vary depending on how strong their buying intent is. For those who haven't yet demonstrated the intent to buy soon, the best content for this stage will tend to be industry insights and thought leadership. These may take the form of blog posts (guest blog posts on leading industry sites can be especially effective for SEO), ebooks, infographics, videos, and industry webinars, perhaps co-sponsored with a leading industry association or featuring a well-known industry expert.

Some offers that have been very successful for my companies and clients include the following:

- Signing up for topic-specific newsletters—not a general newsletter

- Industry-specific materials such as waivers, prescription forms, business cards, etc.

- Free samples

- New product announcements that are related to current events

- Materials designed to empower the prospect's customers— customer-facing handouts, research papers that answer FAQs, etc.

- Comparison grids or charts

- For regulated industries, state-specific information in an easily digestible format

- Ad specialty items—highlighters, hand sanitizer, socks, etc.

- Infographics

- Virtual learning opportunities, ecourses, and ebooks

- Profitability or ROI calculators

The acquisition stage is when you can build your own list of opt-in contacts with emails. While acquired lists are rarely effective, lists of people who have opted in can be very valuable. You'll want to nurture them with new messages regularly. This cadence will depend on your audience and market. Some markets are used to and expect more communication, both direct-sell-based and content-based, while other markets prefer less frequent interaction.

For those who demonstrate a strong intent to buy, take them right to your landing pages where they can close. Some will be almost but not fully ready, and for them, you'll use content about the details and superiority of your offering to move them to buy. In the next chapter, I go over many tactics to help you achieve this.

And don't lose sight of the second tactic—the Lifetime Value Framework. All this has to be done within your program's allowable cost per lead (CPL). If you're generating your leads and therefore sales for less than that, you can boost your budget and get more leads! If your leads and sales are costing too much, though, you need to evaluate your media strategy and offers and possibly cut your program back to get it within your maximum CPL.

USING THE LIFETIME VALUE FRAMEWORK IN THE ACQUISITION STAGE

In the acquisition stage, cost per thousand impressions (CPM) is important, but the key LVF metric is cost per lead (CPL). Outperformers use it as the guardrail that will drive their activities.

To determine your CPL, you need to work backward as described in Chapter 2. How many new customers do you need to close this year? What percentage of leads on average or from a specific campaign will you convert into customers? What percentage of the total addressable market (TAM), therefore, do you need to make leads, and what can you spend to do that?

As you're managing these campaigns, if you're running below your allowable CPL, you may be leaving business on the table, so increase your campaign spending to maximize your number of leads.

If you're running above the CPL, you need to either reduce your spending or optimize your campaigns and offers to get more leads from them.

And if you're running right at the CPL, keep up the good work with constant monitoring and minor adjustments. It may be time to launch a new campaign utilizing a different marketing mix to compare results.

This is complicated by the fact that some of your campaigns will be for brand building or building a content library that will be evergreen for SEO, while other performance-oriented campaigns will have specific CTAs designed to get people to sign up and give you their contact information now.

Remember HubSpot, that extreme case of content marketing mentioned in Chapter 4? They have spent tens of millions of dollars on content in the past 15+ years. As a result, my search on SEMrush estimates that they get six million visits a month from organic search, which would cost them $24 million per month to recreate—if that's even possible. That's close to $300 million in value annually!

Keywords **1.6M** 4.75% | Traffic **6M** 7.89% | Traffic Cost **$24.1M** 5.91%

Although, as also mentioned before, many of these visitors are searching for such general industry keywords as "famous quotes," "Facebook," and "Google Docs," so they aren't likely to be customers soon.

HubSpot has quite a few rankings at the top of page one, although most are lower or on later pages.

Most companies have a SERP distribution like that. One of the few to reverse it is Amazon, which has an almost unimaginable number of top three rankings and gets even greater value from organic search as a result.

Much of your content will have negative value initially. Very few of your pieces will get a coveted top three position on page one, where the majority of clicks happen, in the first six to twelve months. Ahrefs reports

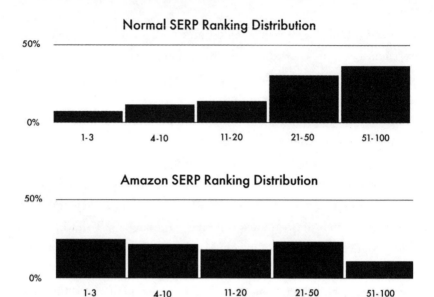

that it typically takes two-plus years for a piece to reach that exalted position, although some industries are easier to get rankings in.[2] There is a famous joke in the SEO world "Where do you hide a dead body online where no one will ever find it? On page two of Google . . ."

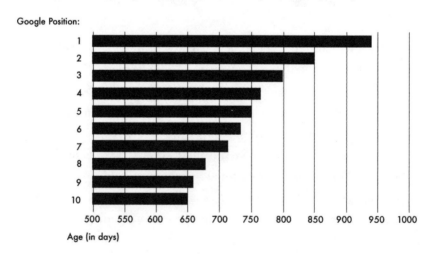

This is why, before creating content, it is so important to start with a keyword analysis of your industry. What are the terms we would love to rank first for in order to convert more customers? What are the terms we would love to rank first for in order to be a thought leader? What are the terms we would love to rank first for in order to get more leads? Once you have identified these terms, you can begin to build out your long-term content strategy with the utilization of, and ranking for, these keywords in mind.

And particular pieces may always have a negative value.

On the other hand, you may have a few all-star pieces that drive most of your visits and leads. And these can be difficult to predict. Here are a few of ours from over the years:

- Those Sanskrit terms in yoga.

- "The Badass Guide to Yoga for Men"—whose success was surprising since the yoga market is mostly women teachers and practitioners.

- A Salon Suite Rental Guide—everything you need to know about renting a salon chair. We did not realize that the industry was trending in that direction. It helped us to rank for those terms and helped us identify those businesses as potential partners.

- Financial services video explanation of claims made versus occurrence form coverage. We did not realize that so many people did not know the difference in coverage types.

People may be in the acquisition stage for months if not years, and additional content and resources—often distributed via email or social media—are how you provide value to them and build your mental availability during this important time, which will eventually help turn them into a lead and then a customer.

Since building this content library is often one of the important steps to long-term acquisition stage success (it will drive down your acquisition costs significantly in the future), it's important to do this and also amortize its cost over its full life rather than just the current month or quarter.

TO GATE OR NOT TO GATE

Critical to acquisition stage success is the production, distribution, and amplification of content. This content serves to build awareness and mental availability for your brand and to generate leads that you will nurture and close in the conversion stage. To get those leads, though, you need to gate some content—put it behind a form that people need to fill in—in order to get people's names and emails, at a minimum.

Gating content has advantages and disadvantages.

The primary advantage of gating content is to get the person's contact information so that you can continue to market and sell to them. Some companies charge thousands of dollars for industry information; you're only asking for their contact information. Gating by itself suggests value. And, of course, generating leads that you can nurture and close can be a great result to report. It helps build confidence within your company in a nascent program.

On the other hand, gating will significantly reduce the number of people who can read—and possibly pass on—your piece. It will make it impossible for Google to crawl and index your content and include it in its search rankings. You may have issues complying with GDPR and CCPA. Your mental availability may grow more slowly.

Robert Rose describes a real-life scenario that probably won't fit neatly into any report.

> When I was the chief marketing officer of a B2B software company, we had one audience member (let's call him Dan) who not only never became a customer, he never once matriculated to a lead or an opportunity. Dan never once spoke, had lunch, or played golf with one of our sales reps. But because Dan was such a fan of our thought leadership program, he

recommended us for more than $1 million of new business in less than two years. Our content helped him get promoted and become a leader in his organization. Dan was one of the primary reasons we became so well known in an industry vertical. He was one of our biggest fans.[3]

If you're doing your multi-channel marketing well, when your salespeople talk to a new prospect who has contacted you and ask, "How did you hear about us?" (as they always should early in the first call), they will hear "I've been following you for years, and now we're ready to act" or "You're everywhere; I figured that I needed to talk to you," among other answers.

Your content marketing will be a balancing act between getting the word out and generating leads.

Because of privacy concerns, some people may be reluctant to give up their contact information. They know what they're signing up for. So, you need to offer something of value to them: a report, ebook, event, etc. You're not going to gate a blog post, so this gated content has to be truly something special. (Yes, all of our content should be special, but this is even more special.)

How will we know if it's valuable enough to people to gate? We experiment.[4] Average conversion rates across a site typically aren't very high, just 2.35%,[5] although they vary by industry from 1.7% (real estate and B2B tech) to 9.3% (professional services).[6] The top 25% of sites have conversion rates of 5.31%. For a "conventional" company and website, you may be knocking it out of the ballpark if you have an offer with an 11.45% conversion rate, as the top 10% of sites do. E-commerce sites sometimes have dramatically higher rates than these.

So, if your offer has a 5–10% or higher conversion rate, that's likely very good and worth keeping it gated. If it's below 3%, on the other hand, you may have an offer that just isn't valuable enough to be gated.

Results may vary for your company and industry. You'll figure out what justifies gating for you. Offers may have a short half-life and become exhausted over time and need updating or replacing. On the other hand, if you are in an industry with rapid turnover, with new members of "Ogilvy's Parade" constantly marching through, your offer may be an evergreen that will be valuable for years.

One way to have your cake and eat it too is to make part of a valuable piece available ungated with a gated offer to download the full piece or report. Others have prospered by making the entire piece available ungated and gating a PDF version for people who want to download it and pass it around.[7]

When gating content, you may want to use progressive profiling. This is when your marketing automation software asks just one or two new questions each time a person downloads some gated content. For the first piece, it may be name and email, then company, then title, and so forth.

TEST, TEST, TEST

The traditional sales mantra is ABC: Always Be Closing.

For marketing, it should be ABT: Always Be Testing.

For multi-channel marketing success, it's critical that you constantly test your channels, offers, and creative and work to optimize them.

- Create goals for your campaigns and tests before starting. In the short run, tests should help you optimize your campaigns; in the long run, they should help you reach the North Star that you and senior management have agreed upon.

- Use statistically significant data. Louis Gudema gives an example where, even with about 30,000 impressions a week, results for a campaign were significantly different in each of the first three weeks.[8] For a national consumer company selling to tens of millions of households, a direct mail test campaign may require 100,000 pieces. What is a statistically significant sample for you?

- Don't test more than three campaign elements at a time. Some people would say to only test one thing at a time, but with multi-variant testing and a large enough sample size, you can successfully test multiple items simultaneously.

- Results are not always as obvious as you may think. While your tests may reveal a "winner," you may find that the "loser" has significant value, too (maybe it's more effective with a particular segment). Sometimes, ads or offers with higher click rates end up having lower ultimate conversion rates. Campaigns that offer price discounts generate short-term sales, but they may also be educating people to only buy when items are on sale. (Many B2B buyers have learned to buy in the last few days of the quarter when they can squeeze quota-desperate salespeople for the best deals.) Dig for insights.

- Apply your learnings to your upcoming campaigns. Period. This isn't an academic exercise.

- Think long term. While your tests may reveal winners and ways to improve your conversion rates, think of each test as a way to better understand your customers. Don't take your results for their face value. Think about the Why behind them. Over time, the cumulative knowledge you accrue from many tests will be more important than what you learn from just one or two.

ATTRIBUTION MODELING

Cross-channel attribution—the ability to identify which channels are contributing to a sale and assigning a specific percentage of attribution and budget—is very challenging. Typically, only large companies with a lot of data can accurately do it. But we have to have an idea of what's working; ZoomInfo says that effective attribution can improve your marketing efficiency by 15–30%.[9]

Smaller companies have attribution capabilities, too.

First, consider the different types of common attribution models and their limits:

- Last click, or last interaction, model gives 100% of the credit for the sale to the last action taken, whether it's clicking on a search ad, social ad, email, or whatever. It's useful, but it may ignore many, many previous interactions that gave the customer the information and confidence to go ahead with buying from you. Avinash Kaushik is more direct about this when he says, "Last click reporting sucks. Because it lies."[10]

- First click/interaction is a model that some B2B companies with large enterprise sales find useful. They may have a three-to-six-month or longer sales cycle, and the deal is ultimately attributable to the sales team, with many interactions along the way. First click may be a way to understand the actions that initially introduced the vendor and produced the most leads.

- Linear attribution gives equal credit to every interaction along the way. This may be more realistic than last click, but essentially, you're throwing up your hands and saying that we don't really know, so everyone gets a participation trophy.

- Position-based attribution gives bigger shares of the credit to the first and last interactions—typically 40% to each—with the rest spread evenly to all other interactions in between.

- Time decay attribution gives most of the credit to the interactions closest to the sale with a declining share of credit the further away from the sale the interaction happened.

- You can also create custom models that better match your situation.

In 2019, Scott Rheinlander from Salesforce wrote that "the jury's still out on the most successful marketing attribution models."[11] If the jury's still out after decades of effort, it will probably stay out because no one model fits all companies and situations.

Gathering the data for attribution modeling can be challenging. People usually engage with brands across multiple devices. They may be using a desktop or laptop at home and a different one at work, a tablet or two, and a phone or two. Can you track them across all of those devices and record the data? This will be made even more challenging in our cookieless future.

And effective attribution modeling requires cooperation across the company, with data being shared between marketing, sales, customer experience, and other areas.

This is further complicated by the different lead times for different marketing channels. We know that email and search ads, for example, typically produce swift results. And they're typically very efficient. If you aren't getting results from them, you'll know pretty soon. Last click attribution is fine for these.

Price promotions, on the other hand, will typically deliver quick, verifiable results. They also will destroy your brand and turn your customers into bargain hunters. (Remember from Chapter 1 that strong brands can charge more and consequently have better margins.)

Content marketing and SEO, though, have long lead times. They may take three to six months or longer to start contributing to your results but in the long run (years) may be great and inexpensive channels. Your results will eventually show up in your time decay model, but don't expect it immediately.

Another attribution challenge is being able to identify incremental sales. If you're entering a new market, this won't be an issue because all your sales are incremental and attributable to marketing. But if your company is already in a market (with considerable brand awareness), how much are your marketing programs driving new, incremental sales? Some major consumer brands found that they could significantly reduce digital advertising without losing any sales.

It is complicated, indeed.

Informal attribution research can be done by doing tests, such as launching some campaigns in just a particular city or geography and tracking results.

Google provides attribution modeling tools in Analytics and Google

Ads. Large marketing suites like those from Adobe and Salesforce, and other software, provide even more sophisticated tools. Give it a shot, and see if it can help you.

If those tools don't help, I usually recommend bringing on an analyst who has experience in either selecting or creating attribution models. They can help you choose the right model off-the-shelf, or they can build a new attribution solution whole cloth, tailoring it to your particular company and your particular campaigns.

In my experience, it's better for SMBs to use an off-the-shelf model. All models involve extraordinary complexity, so building a custom one can be both time-intensive and costly. Meanwhile, for most SMBs, off-the-shelf models do a great job of delivering clear, reliable, actionable data.

Pro tip: you may find it useful to compare attribution models against one another to find what is the best application for your business. It is very useful to compare the results of both historic and current campaigns across models in order to decide which has a more accurate picture based on the financial results you are seeing.

WHEN A COMPETITOR KILLS A CHANNEL

Sometimes companies backed by VCs are focused on one thing and one thing only: growth.

And mostly they don't care what it costs.

As a result, they may undertake campaign practices that are irrational to those of us who want and need to operate profitably. Specifically, they'll pay way too much for leads and conversions.

I've seen this take the form of companies overbidding on search keywords, for example. Or maxing out the pay per click channel by going for 100% impression share. Or a startup with no profitability showing up with a 40×40 booth at the industry's largest tradeshow.

In these situations, they'll be paying way more for a customer than they can make from them. That's their problem; don't make it yours.

If a channel is too expensive, go elsewhere until that channel returns to the realm of reason. If PPC is so expensive that you can't be profitable using it, don't use it, or use it within the realm of your customer acquisition cost when you can. But keep your eye on it. At some point—maybe a few months, maybe much longer—the competitor will change their strategy or go out of business or whatever, and the channel will return to its senses. And then you can start to use it.

CASE STUDY—DON'T DO THIS

This is a negative case study, an example of "don't do this."

I was working with a company (which shall remain nameless for reasons that will be obvious) in the camping/guns/survival industry.

Their acquisition stage programs were not very efficient for a number of reasons, and as a result, they were not getting nearly as many leads as they should have for their efforts. In other words, their cost per lead was too high. But they didn't need to cut their acquisition budget, they needed to improve their programs. Often, the best way to get more budget is to simply reallocate.

First, they weren't segmenting, even in the easiest ways. They weren't segmenting between customers and prospective customers. Or between the highest and lowest value customers. Or between those with current outstanding orders and those who weren't waiting for an order to arrive.

So, in the early days of COVID when they were experiencing production and shipping delays, everyone—customers with orders, customers without orders, and prospective customers—was getting emails apologizing for delays in the shipment of orders. This hurt sales. When they segmented and only sent those to customers with orders outstanding, sales immediately increased.

They were committing random acts of marketing. As you know, I advocate multi-channel marketing, but they were everywhere, and not in an informed, productive, synergistic way. They had multiple websites and too many social accounts (some active, some dormant). Their paid PPC, search, and social ads were ineffective because of poor keyword analysis and targeting.

Again, you know that rule #1 is that you're not marketing to yourself. You need to understand your customer and create marketing that will reach and move them. However, one of this company's owners liked cigars and so, on the assumption that all of their male customers liked cigars, and maybe even a few of their female ones, they created a line of branded cigars and began to put them in every order. Every. Single. Order.

You might look at this and think that there was a lot of low-hanging fruit, but it was worse than that. The rotting fruit was all over the ground.

The road to far more leads was clear:

- Segment and use email marketing better

- Consolidate the websites[12]

- Shut down the dormant social sites and consolidate the remaining

- Undertake keyword research, including the top keywords of their competitors, and run a well-targeted PPC program; test multiple offers and landing pages

- Target social ads using interests

- Use remarketing ads

- Eliminate overpriced print ads

- Stop sending out cigars with every order

They saved money (no more cigars or overpriced print) while significantly improving their results.

FIVE-TACTIC ACQUISITION

In the end, acquisition becomes perhaps the best proving ground for the Five-Tactic Marketing Framework. More than any other funnel stage, it requires us to fire on all cylinders at once. Given the complexity of the challenge, it's no wonder that single-tactic marketing strategies peter out, landing companies in sales plateaus and undermining profitability.

To achieve high performance during acquisition, you have to deploy all five tactics in unison. Because the mouth of the funnel is so wide, encompassing the full range of targets from no intent to high intent, you have to use both brand marketing and performance marketing (tactic #1). That's how you get impressions, build brand awareness, foster trust, and develop leads.

Meanwhile, tactic #2—the Lifetime Value Framework—governs execution, telling us what to spend and how to measure. Ultimately, we need to launch all of these acquisition efforts via integrated, multi-channel campaigns, becoming deeply strategic about *whom* we're speaking to (tactic #3) and *where* we're speaking to them (tactic #4).

Only through all five tactics can we achieve maximized results.

Which, of course, brings us to tactic #5 . . .

AI USE CASES: ACQUISITION ENABLED BY AI

Creation
Campaign Ideation

As we've seen before, some of generative AI's greatest contributions come during brainstorming. Whether you're brand building for low-intent leads, rolling out thought leadership for medium-intent leads, or funneling high-intent leads straight to the point of sale, AI can help you ideate on possible approaches. And if you feed it criteria like target market, seasonality, past performance, and price point, the AI will take all of those factors into consideration. Some models can process up to 200 pages of context that can help inform the response to the prompt!

Campaign Material Creation

Another returning use case. Generative AI can draft calls to action, design landing pages, and write thought leadership. It can build comparison charts, design infographics, and translate technical industry jargon into simple, consumer-facing copy. Whatever you need created, generative AI should be your first stop for first drafts.

Operation

Social Listening

Digital marketers have long used listening software to log and examine brand-related conversations across social platforms. Now, AI-powered tools are augmenting that work, labeling topics, tracking trends, and identifying key influencers. In a nutshell, AI-powered tools present the facts with deeper context, digging past keywords to identify big ideas. Some AIs also use computer vision to cast a wider net, capturing video and photos in addition to text. This has become increasingly vital given the dominance of visual media online.

Sentiment Analysis

This is another augmentation of traditional social listening software. Some AI tools log not only what's being said, but also *how* it's being said—positively or negatively. By scoring social sentiment, these tools help SMBs quickly identify their biggest strengths as well as their most dire liabilities.

Pinpoint Acquisition Allowables

Use AI to predict order values. Then, based on those order values, reverse engineer individual acquisition allowables for each customer. This is achieved using "propensity models," which draw on web history, user characteristics, and first-party data to predict the likelihood of a purchase, the value of a purchase, and/or the frequency of future purchases—all calculated specifically for individual users. Ultimately, these individual allowables inform PPC and other kinds of AI-driven, pinpoint marketing. You can then continue training the AI over time, giving it feedback on how past predictions panned out.

Optimization

Performance Analysis

Finally, use data-oriented AIs to analyze campaign *performance* and identify key trends. Then leverage these insights to fine-tune acquisition campaigns for optimal performance.

CHAPTER 6

CONVERSION

Because the purpose of business is to create a customer,
the business enterprise has two—and only two—basic
functions: marketing and innovation. Marketing and
innovation produce results; all the rest are costs.

—PETER DRUCKER[1]

Our journey down the funnel continues. After a person or company becomes a lead, they enter the conversion stage. The single goal of the conversion stage is to make them a customer. This may take minutes, months, or years. And it will require all five tactics of our Five-Tactic Marketing Framework.

THE KEYS TO CONVERSION

In the conversion stage, the key Lifetime Value Framework metric is cost per acquisition (CPA). While that may seem straightforward enough, the CPA may vary by segment, product, and other factors. Each may have its own distinct customer lifetime value (CLV), supporting different CPAs.

For example, if we think back to the differences between Home Depot's commercial customers (contractors) and its independent consumers (homeowners), the contractors will certainly have an average CLV 100–1,000+ times higher than the typical homeowner. And among those contractors, there will be multiple segments, too. Of course, Home Depot would need to market differently to them and use different success metrics.

A key driver of conversion stage activities is the demonstrated intent of the customer. The most certain initial indicator of their degree of intent is what kind of campaign generated the prospect. For example, a prospect who downloaded a white paper, general industry insights, or an infographic is low intent. One who wants to schedule a demo is medium intent. One who was generated by high-intent search ads is, of course, high intent. While, in general, in this stage, we may provide two pieces of valuable content to each closing message, we will switch that ratio for the high-intent customer.

The very highest intent customer is one who has abandoned a shopping cart. For them, we use 100% closing messages and in a quite urgent cadence. Initially, we remind them to come back. If that doesn't quickly work, we can provide an incentive. The sequence might be something like this:

- Email sent out within minutes or hours of abandoning the cart (the precise time frame varies by business)

- Using programmatic to target them with online display and PPC ads

- After no action in 24 to 48 hours, an email with an incentive

- After no more than 48 hours, a phone outreach

Obviously, having a sales rep call is the most expensive conversion effort, so we save it for last. But if that's what it takes to close the sale and you can afford it based on CLV, you should do it. In some industries, that personal connection is especially important. Pro tip: study the new Telephone Consumer Protection Act laws that are scheduled to go into effect over the next couple of years. It can be very costly to violate regulations when attempting to contact prospective customers by phone or text.

Note that while you may be worried that you're overcommunicating or inundating your customers with communications, you can rest assured:

you most likely aren't doing anything of the kind. Most companies don't have this marketing automation functionality, so your conversion push will likely feel novel and passionate, not tired and spammy.

Also, test everything! If you turn on these abandoned-cart closers, and the data shows that it's negatively impacting your brand or sales, then you have your answer. (Although, again, this probably won't happen.)

Finally, don't use third-party firms for these closing conversations. In my experience, they rarely are knowledgeable enough. They are likely to be ineffective and even harmful.

In addition to different strategies based on the level of intent, you'll also want to use different messages and content. For those with low-to-medium intent, continue to add value. Inform them about the industry with

- ebooks

- white papers

- videos

- blog posts

- infographics

- and other information

Occasionally, mix in information about your offering and the value it can provide.

As someone shows deeper intent, you can give them more information specifically about your offering, which will vary by industry. It may be

- an ROI calculator

- competitive grid

- tech specs

- and—if needed—the opportunity for a demo or conversation with a company rep

Reserve a special place in your messaging to high-intent people for voice of the customer (VOC) materials. Generally, potential customers want to hear more about how great we are from our customers than from us. Frankly, they trust them more. That's why online reviews are so important and why it's important to build up your online reviews. So be sure to include VOC content. Case studies are especially impactful for this purpose.

Some people will move right up from low intent to medium to high and a sale. Some may go in the opposite direction. We can't know everything that's going on inside their decision-making process. If they move from high to low, it may mean that conditions changed at their company, new people came in, budgets changed, and what was a high priority isn't now. Or it may mean they bought from a competitor. You can try to find out if a potential sale is worth enough—this is a gold mine of information if they'll tell you. Most won't. But in any case, if they are showing less intent, then change their lead score to reflect that and change how you're interacting with them.

— *SIDEBAR* —

HANDING LEADS OVER TO SALES

In some cases, especially larger deals, you may turn a lead over to sales to close. That sales process itself may go on for weeks or months.

In most cases, salespeople will want you to simultaneously remove the lead from your marketing nurture campaigns. They will want to use more personalized communications and content that addresses the specific situation and objections of that lead. They'll be concerned that the lead may see anything else from your company as a nuisance or just confusing. That would be a poor customer experience (CX), and I talk more about the importance of CX shortly.

To help sales close the deal, you'll need to enable salespeople with the content that they need. Some of this may be the same content that you're using in your conversion stage campaigns, but other content may be different or customizable.

And, by the way, make sure that leads actually are being turned over to sales. When preparing for a trade show with one client, I asked what results they had produced from the leads of the show the year before. They told me that while they had generated lots of leads at last year's trade show, they had never turned those leads over to sales. That is unacceptable. Then they asked us to help them with ANOTHER lead generation campaign at the next year's trade show. Before we took that on, I insisted that the CEO show us their plan to turn the leads over to sales after the show. It is not enough to generate leads; you must convert them!

CONVERSION RATE OPTIMIZATION (CRO) STRATEGIES

For very little money, often for free, you can dramatically improve your conversion results—by 50–100% or more—with better conversion tactics. That's closing twice as many deals or more and dramatically reducing your cost per acquisition for zero additional dollars. You can't ignore this. Act now!

Conversion rate optimization (CRO) involves such factors as offers, wording, cadence of messages, landing page layout and design, and financing options.

Behavioral scientists have researched the impact of different CRO strategies for decades. It is well worth studying what they have learned. Most of these strategies are based on the fact that we buy with emotion and justify with logic, and CRO strategies bypass our logical brain to get our emotional, quick, decision-making brain to act.

Daniel Kahneman writes extensively about framing: the context in which you receive information can have a significant effect on how you act. For example, he writes, "Cold cuts described as '90% fat-free' are more attractive than when they are described as '10% fat.'"[2]

Framing is used to good effect by many companies' pricing pages. This is the pricing page for Zoho CRM.

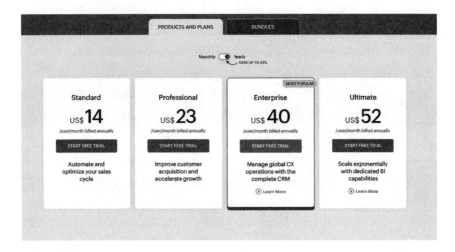

At the top, you can toggle between monthly and yearly pricing.[3] It's not uncommon on SaaS sites to see a "most popular" callout next to a middle option—when given three or four choices, people tend to choose a middle one. And a free trial is offered at every level.

Robert Cialdini describes six key principles of persuasion in his classic *Influence*:[4]

- Reciprocity: Give something to make the customer feel that they owe you something. Your valuable content contributes to this; what else can? I give an example of how I used reciprocity in this chapter's Case Study section at the end.

- Commitment and consistency: Once people make a small commitment, they're more likely to follow through. Salespeople use this when asking leads a few small questions with a likely "yes" answer to warm them up for the close. This is sometimes called getting a "micro-yes."

- Social proof: Using numbers of customers ("billions of hamburgers sold" or "over 300,000 newsletter subscribers") and reviews to create trust and a kind of bandwagon effect.

- Liking: People are more apt to be influenced and persuaded by those they like. So use likable people and images in your campaigns.

- Authority: Some people with authority in their field have more sway than others. These could be experts, executives, or influencers.

- Scarcity: People want what they can't have, so use scarcity ("just five left") and urgency ("24 hours to act").

Nancy Harhut builds on Cialdini with several additional strategies, including the following, to name just a few:[5]

- Storytelling: people relate to stories better than to facts and figures, remember them longer, and stories are a great way to create an emotional connection with a customer.

- Loss aversion: people put a greater weight on losing than gaining; so if you can position your offer as a way of avoiding loss, it is more likely to be successful.

- Reasoning: use the word "because" because if people are given almost any reason for a requested action, they are much more likely to take it.

There is more, much more. So, study the classics of behavioral science and performance marketing, and put their insights to good (profitable) use.[6]

Your landing page design can, again, have a big impact on your results at no cost: you're going to design it somehow, you might as well do it right and get a lot more business from it.

A simple mistake I see all the time is a landing page with the headline and text above the fold and the form starting below it; many people won't realize that the page has a form, and so they won't fill it out. By simply testing how the landing page would perform if the text was on the left and the form on the right, above the fold, they might greatly increase their conversion rate.

Even seemingly small changes like the color of buttons, a different image, and the use of a video can have sizeable impacts on your conversion rate.

For one client's customer base, we tested using emojis in the subject line. Open rates *decreased* by 68%. Wow—message received.

All of your people must buy into this approach and the primacy of closing the deal. When we post a job opening for a creative role in our firm, the first line of the description is, "If it doesn't sell, it's art, and we don't make art." That weeds out most of the creatives who are more interested in form than function and, therefore, wouldn't be happy working with us.

Remember in Chapter 4, I mentioned that the offer is far more important than the creative, which I've been talking about here. A great offer can produce a 10X improvement in responses compared to these creative changes.

For another client's customer base, we created a raffle with thousands of dollars in prizes. The landing page saw over 10,000 unique visitors with 4,749 signing up for the raffle.

Payment terms are one type of offer. I mentioned Zoho has options for a monthly fee or an annual one whose monthly average rates would be lower. You can offer four easy payments or whatever makes sense for you. The important thing is that you provide options; give customers a choice. As Nancy Harhut says, "You're always free to . . ." are four of the most powerful words in sales.[7]

You will want to explore various pricing models. As I mentioned earlier, people tend to take the middle option. This is known as "decoy pricing" or "the decoy effect."[8] And there are many ways to increase the profitability of that middle option. With decoy pricing, you strategically create a low-value package, a middle package, and a high-value package. The key is that the middle-value package is priced significantly closer to the high-value package than to the low. This has been shown to dramatically increase conversion rates for the high- and middle-value packages.

In addition to your language and offer, consider your cadence of messages. While daily emails always had a bad rap, 10 years ago they could have been effective. But since we get so many commercial emails, solicited and unsolicited, in many cases now companies have moved to weekly or a couple of times a week.

We conducted a survey of customers for a company and found that most thought that they were receiving too many email promos and newsletters. We changed the cadence of messages from weekly promos and newsletters to a promo every other week while retaining the weekly newsletter. We went from eight to ten messages a month to six. Open rates increased by 34%. Even open rates for non-members increased by 20.5%. Although conversion rates didn't change, this increase in opens produced a significant increase in sales.

You can split your list into segments and test which cadence is most effective for you.

Some CRO strategies will be more effective with low-cost offers sold to one person (which may be more like an impulse purchase) than for higher-cost items that are decided on by a buying team of several people. Over the weeks and months of discussions by the buying team, the wording or layout of your landing page is not going to have much of an impact; finance options may.

As always, it's all about understanding the customer. What works in one industry may fall flat in another. Outperformers approach multi-channel performance marketing with an attitude of experimentation and are prepared to be surprised. Test new things—even moonshots—that couldn't possibly work. You might be pleasantly surprised.

BUILDING A GREAT CUSTOMER EXPERIENCE

I mentioned before that Steve Jobs considered every interaction that a brand has with a customer and potential customer as an opportunity to contribute to a great customer experience. After all, for most customers, your customer experience (CX) will essentially define your brand for them.

Jobs had a long-standing interest in the retail experience.[9] When vacationing with his wife, he would often go into luxury brand stores like Gucci and Prada. But he didn't just walk around. He'd make mental notes of every bit of design and architecture and actively grill employees on why the store was laid out like it was, how they interacted with customers, and how the purchase went. These were not dreary, crowded computer stores, and with this high-end retail approach, they were able to sell very expensive items indeed. Could it work for computers?

After Jobs returned to Apple in the late 1990s, he hired Target's vice president of merchandising, Ron Johnson, to create a unique, effective, and on-brand shopping experience for Apple. Johnson spent weeks reconsidering every aspect of the retail customer experience. Eventually, they set up a prototype store in a warehouse and spent months working out the design. In May 2001, they opened the first stores. While the business press ridiculed the stores that violated so many retail norms, the customers loved them. And in addition to being a source of considerable sales and customer support, the 500+ stores provide a huge lift to the Apple brand.

One of the greatest compliments was when Microsoft opened its stores and essentially copied the design of the Apple stores.

Similarly, every interaction in the acquisition, conversion, and customer retention stages must contribute to that great CX. Anything that doesn't, detracts from it.

All of your outreach in the acquisition and conversion stages must be on-brand, honest, and ethical. Those behavior science hacks that I mentioned before aren't ways to trick people into buying something that they don't want or need; that would be a very poor long-term business strategy.

They are ways to optimize our results from customers who can get value from our offerings. It should be a win-win.

The Five Es of Customer Experience are as follows:

- Entice: How do customers first hear of us?

- Enter: What's their initial experience?

- Engage: How do we interact with them as we do business with them (which begins with closing the sale)?

- Exit: What is the end of their experience with us like?

- Extend: How do we encourage repeat business and a longer relationship?

In the acquisition and conversion stages, we're enticing, entering, and engaging the customer. In the customer retention stage, we're focused on extending the customer relationship and increasing the customer lifetime value. In this book, I'm not concerned with the customer's exit—in a perfect world, they would never truly exit.

While people increasingly seek a salesperson-free experience, is that what your customers want? Or do they want people who will quickly and knowledgeably answer their questions and make it easy to make a purchase?

It is astonishing how the customer experiences of some websites and apps fail. Honestly, it's hard to imagine that anyone in the company went through them even once. That is a minimum. I cannot tell you how many times I have been in a conference room and asked the executives if they have ever called into their business's customer-facing automated phone system (IVR). Most of the time, they don't even know what I am talking about. So, I call their business from the conference room phone. Most of the time, we hang up, all agreeing that the experience must be dramatically improved.

Ideal customer experiences are created through close collaborations with the customers themselves over time.

A key moment in CX is when your product first arrives. In the computer industry, they spent considerable effort creating a great OOBE—Out of Box Experience—so people could quickly and without hassle start using their new computer. Not to belabor Apple, but a great example of that is when you buy a new iPad. It arrives in an elegant box, the instructions are clear, and if you have an old iPad, it'll automatically move over all of your apps and files if you want it to. Easy peasy. It was so incredibly novel when they first did it; now everyone else tries to do it, too.

Personal customer support may be especially important for satisfying customers and upselling them. People want to be able to easily reach a support rep and not encounter an endless sequence of phone prompts. Support is a key opportunity to increase your customer lifetime value, after all, so it behooves you to get it right.

I'm sure that you've encountered plenty of great customer experiences (Apple, JetBlue, Southwest Air, Amazon) and plenty of terrible ones (cable companies, health insurers, internet service providers). Think about how JetBlue and Southwest make it more fun to fly or how Amazon makes it so easy to order and return an item.

The late Tony Hsieh, Zappos co-founder and CEO, said that they learned early on that their best customers were those who *returned* their orders. They had tested Zappos' no-cost, no-hassle, 365-returns policy, found that it was true, and so they then trusted Zappos as a site without risk and became loyal customers.[10]

Over the past 25 years, the banking industry has transformed its CX from "banker's hours" (with early closings on Wednesdays) to longer hours, smart ATMs, and the ability to make deposits and conduct many other transactions using a mobile app.

In the early days of Amazon, Jeff Bezos had an empty chair in every meeting. It represented the customer. He wanted his people to always be thinking about what they could do for that customer. He has said repeatedly, "Our goal is to be earth's most customer-centric company."[11] Once again, be like Amazon.

COMMON MISTAKES

Some of the mistakes I see companies making that greatly depress their conversion stage results include the following:

- Poor user interfaces (UI): It's not easy and obvious how to use their site or app and make the purchase. You should have 20–50 people test a site or app before it goes live. Watch them as they try it and see where they get hung up. Go through the process yourself to begin with.

- Poor user experience (UX): Have you ever secret-shopped your site or company? Ever called the support center? Signed up for a newsletter? What's it like to do business with you? Even if someone only signs up for a newsletter, they want confirmation of it.

- Thinking that they are their customers: What appeals to you will very rarely be what appeals to your customers. Don't assume that you know what will appeal; do the hard work to find out.

- Treating every lead the same: They aren't all the same, and they need to be treated (very) differently based on the level of intent.

- Insufficient urgency for high-intent leads: Your high-intent prospects are your gold leads. You must do everything you can to close them in 24 to 48 hours before they go on to something else. Because something else is always just a click away.

Avoid the Last Click Error

As I discussed in the previous chapter, last click attribution can be useful for some channels like search ads. But people may be in the conversion stage for a long time. They'll be getting a lot of emails and other content from you. They may visit your website, read your blog, view your YouTube channel, and attend your events. And you may send many closing messages to them before they buy.

So don't make the mistake of giving all the credit to the one message that finally closed them. It was likely a confluence of many interactions that produced the sale.

CASE STUDY—WAKE UP AND SMELL THE ROSES

There are all sorts of ways—both digital and analog—to increase conversion rates.

Partnerships with trade associations are often a major driver of business for the companies that I own and work with. But to get access to their thousands of members, we first need to connect with just one person at the association who can green-light the deal. This sometimes calls for out-of-the-box analog sales strategies.

In one case, we used the reciprocity principle when we were having trouble (despite repeated attempts) getting the meeting. We literally sent the person $5,000 worth of roses. Her office was filled to the brim with roses. We had commanded her attention, and she decided to reciprocate and talk with us. It didn't take long for her to recognize the potential opportunity. The partnership was sealed, and we both profited from the results.

Two notes: our operations people went nuts when they saw an expense report with $5,000 for flowers. But senior management understood it. And, if you do this, make sure first that the person isn't allergic to flowers!

In other cases, we've sent a person an official-looking, unsigned check made out to their company for a large amount that we thought we could produce for them, with the message, "Wouldn't you like us to generate this for you?" It gets across the scale of the opportunity and often results in a meeting.

When we know a person has children, we may send them a radio-controlled car or helicopter without the remote. The accompanying letter says that when we meet with them, we'll bring the remote along.

We'll do anything ethical to get that meeting.

However, we once were trying to get a meeting with a senior partnership executive when this backfired. We tried calling, emailing, and finding him at conferences—nothing worked. So we looked at his Facebook account and

discovered that he was really into the architecture of a certain period and also certain bands. We put together a personalized care package for him with gifts related to those interests and a handwritten note, and we sent it to him. We didn't get any response and learned later that he thought that it was kind of overbearing and a bit creepy. It was too much for him. So not only did we not get the meeting, but we also put a damper on the relationship.

Bear in mind that while these analog strategies might sound more sensational than digital conversion rate optimization, digital CRO is still crucial. Here's an example from one of our own businesses, where we approached digital CRO quite clinically, and got terrific results.

We tested a single, long form versus an accordion style that moved you through three sections. The image on the previous page is the original, very long form.

We tested several iterations. Ultimately, the much shorter form in three sections with an accordion design (shown on the next page) produced a 27% higher conversion rate.

We generated far more business just by changing the design of the form and simultaneously reducing the testimonials and social proof elements.

That cost virtually nothing and produced great results. An almost infinite ROI.

MULTI-TACTIC CONVERSION

Given everything there is to consider here, it's no wonder that single-tactic marketing regularly hits plateaus and underperforms. As with acquisition, successful, reliable, high-performance conversion requires a five-tactic approach.

It's clear at first glance that conversion is the ultimate venue for performance marketing (tactic #1); this is precisely the moment when urgent calls to action matter most. But performance marketing alone is not sufficient. It must be shored up through brand marketing (tactic #1), and it must get an integrated deployment across all appropriate channels (tactic #4) informed by deep customer understanding (tactic #3).

MASSAGE MAGAZINE
INSURANCE PLUS+

Secure Application

1. Configure Your Liability Policy ▾

Choose Your Profession

Select your main profession and add any additional modalities or disciplines you would like coverage for. Please select Health Coach as your primary modality in the drop-down below for Health Coach coverage.

| Massage ▲▼ |

☐ Add additional secondary practices or disciplines

Choose Your Insurance Plus Options

| 06/15/2024 | through 6/15/2025

⦿ $169 today or as low as $15.49/mo for 12 months Insurance Plus Professional Rate

◯ $299 today or as low as $27.41/mo for 12 months Two Year Insurance Plus Professional Rate

◯ $49 Insurance Plus Student Rate

◯ $59 Continuing Education Package (No Insurance)

◯ $159 today or as low as $14.58/mo for 12 months Insurance Plus Part-time Rate

☐ **NEW: Add microblading coverage for only $499.**

Add Additional Businesses to Your Policy

Please click the "Add Additional Businesses" link below to add additional businesses to your policy. Any additional businesses you add will protect them from any liability that might arise from your work. As an example, if you're an independent trainer going into different gyms to train, you'll likely want to add these places of work to your policy. Cost per additional business: $10 for 1 year and $15.95 for a 2 year policy.

Unlimited Additional Businesses Package

Throughout the span of your policy, you may likely have to add additional businesses. The cost of adding new businesses can add up. Why not save this expense by purchasing the **Unlimited Additional Businesses Package**?

☐ $30 Unlimited Additional Insureds

| Add Additional Businesses |

Online CEUs that cater to your interests, your budget, and your time. Fulfill your state's online CE requirements with **100% NCBTMB-approved** courses. MassageCEU.com is approved by the National Certification Board for Therapeutic Massage and Bodywork (NCBTMB) as a continuing education Approved Provider. Learn more.

⦿ Unlimited Massage CEs Package Included Per Year

NEXT

2. Your Information ▸

3. Review and Checkout ▸

Meanwhile, none of this will work if we don't keep our eye on the ball: profits. For this reason, the metrics of the Lifetime Value Framework are vital here (tactic #2).

And finally, there's the fifth tactic—crucial AI applications—which we'll tackle in just a moment.

Once again, the central assertion of this book stands: all the tools you need for maximized marketing campaigns are already out there. The trick is simply to use them all—and to deploy them in harmony.

AI USE CASES: CONVERSION ENABLED BY AI

Creation

Campaign Ideation

As is often the case, generative AI will be our first port of call, helping us dream up conversion campaigns. You can use these tools first to ideate on overall campaign strategy—for instance, identifying options for abandoned cart messaging and content-based activations. Then, once you've zeroed in on an overall strategy, generative AI can help you further ideate on creative direction. As always, feed the AI data on your business to get bespoke, context-specific recommendations.

Campaign Material Creation

Once you've got a clear direction, use generative AI to create campaign materials like call scripts, abandoned cart emails, and conversion-oriented blog posts. Note that some companies now use generative AI to fabricate voice of the customer content as well—things like reviews and testimonials. This is illegal and unethical. As we discussed earlier in this chapter, tricking people into buying your product is a poor long-term business strategy.

Personalization

Long gone are the days when anyone was impressed by "Dear [Name]." AI radically boosts opportunities to personalize messaging, expanding both the data you can draw on and the magnitude of personalization you can perform. Before the AI boom, we were already able to capture things like location, browser history, purchase history, current online activity, social media posts, and customer support interactions. But, for a long time, it wasn't practical to collect, analyze, and utilize all of that available data on any one prospect. Now, with AI, you can affordably use this data to personalize emails, ads, and even whole websites, delivering the right content and the right recommendations, at the right time of day, in the right tone of voice for that one individual.

Web Development

This is a particular type of material creation that deserves special mention. Tap an AI to design and build your landing pages, as well as other web-based assets. If you need a specific functionality coded, you can also have an AI write that script. Once again, the more context you input, the more helpful the AI's outputs will become.

Software Development

As with web development, AI can create and deploy new tools or solutions to improve customer experience. This includes fixing bugs in your existing proprietary software, as well as adding new features.

Customer Service

Ensure accurate, rapid responses by training an AI chatbot on your knowledge base and/or other key materials. Once trained, the chatbot can offer both external support (to customers) and internal support (to your customer service reps), instantly and simultaneously responding to a swarm of queries for which no single person could retain all the answers.

Operation
Lead Scoring/Segmentation

During conversion, AI continues to be a great tool for segmentation and lead scoring. As in other domains, these tools have the power to study huge collections of data, identify hidden trends, and act on them. It can be particularly powerful to have your AI compare existing customers with new leads and score/segment based on similarities. For example, your AI might observe that the majority of existing customers came in via pay per click; it might then suggest a higher score for new leads who've likewise been captured via PPC.

Marketing Automation

Simple marketing automations have been prolific for some time now—for instance, sending welcome emails to leads when they subscribe to newsletters. AIs empower us to step up our game, implementing more complex, more targeted automations. Most obviously, these tools can conduct personalized messaging and outreach based on segmentation and user action, as covered in "Personalization" earlier. But the capabilities go much deeper, too. You can also automate deployment of integrated campaigns, directing the AI to recalibrate spend or launch whole new activations in real time based on current performance.

Conversion Rate Optimization

Throughout any given campaign, you and your team will, of course, be monitoring performance, looking for opportunities to improve conversion rates. AI tools can help, often making observations and recommendations that humans would miss. They do this by monitoring and analyzing prospects' digital behaviors in real time. Then they recommend changes to optimize UX, UI, and other campaign elements.

Optimization
Price Modeling

Ask your AI to suggest pricing based on product type, competitive landscape, and other context. Then use that same tool to model and test pricing structures, tracking real-time data on conversion and financials. The AI will optimize for conversion rate and/or profitability at your direction.

CHAPTER 7

CUSTOMER RETENTION AND UPSELL

The better the buyer-seller relationship, the greater the profit.
—LESTER WUNDERMAN, *Being Direct*[1]

Once the prospect becomes a customer, your work is not over. You then have the opportunity to increase their customer lifetime value (CLV). When you increase CLV, the higher profits (you didn't have to spend as many marketing dollars to generate them) not only drop to your bottom line, but you can also increase how much you spend to acquire leads and convert them into customers.

IMPROVING YOUR CUSTOMER EXPERIENCE

A key method for increasing CLV is by improving your customer experience (CX). In the previous chapter, I went over the Five Es of CX:

- Entice: How do customers first hear of us?

- Enter: What's their initial experience?

- Engage: How do we interact with them as we do business with them (which begins with closing the sale)?

- Exit: What is the end of their experience with us like?

- Extend: How do we encourage repeat business and a longer relationship?

The second, third, and fifth Es—Enter, Engage, and Extend—are all relevant to this phase.

Enter: The first step to a successful customer relationship is to stop marketing to them like they haven't bought from you but still might. What's more annoying than seeing remarketing ads and other marketing for something that you've already bought? To eliminate this type of remarketing, you may need to use a "burn pixel" on a thank you page. This is a web-based tool that will help you track who's made a purchase.

How are you onboarding new customers? Are you providing them with all the information they need? Are you making it easy for them? If you're selling an insurance package, the hope is that they'll never need it. But if you're selling something like software that they expect to use regularly, you need to ask yourself how to get them to Wow! more quickly. Because if they don't get to Wow!, they may fall into that set of customers who are more likely to cancel than to stay.

Customers will certainly want different content than prospects. You no longer need to educate and convince them on why they need your product, now you need to educate them on how to get the most out of it. How can you turn your new customers into expert users? Do you need to send out a series of emails over the first few weeks with tips and best practices? Do you need to make phone support available only during business hours or 24/7? Does each new customer need a customer success rep assigned to them with regular meetings?

Engage: When engaging, you will extend the practices that you started in the Enter stage.

Is it even easier for existing customers to order from you? Can they set up automatic, repeat, timed purchases—like "send me this every four months"? Can they see a history of their orders and relationships (you have the data in your systems)? Could you fast-track new purchases for existing customers?

Should you create an online community of users? Your customers may be faster and better at answering questions about your products than your people are. Should you have an annual in-person conference for your customers? Usually, only your happiest customers will attend, and that's okay: those are the ones whom you can deepen your relationship with and turn into advocates.

I organize retention and upsell offerings into three categories:

1. Pure value added—services, support, resources, etc.—that may be useful for the customer (like the AmEx OPEN Forum described shortly)

2. Products and services that make the solution they bought even more valuable for them

3. New offerings, which may or may not add value to the original purchase but would be valuable in and of themselves for the customer

Build a complete customer experience that takes advantage of all three of these. But be tasteful: you don't want to start selling again to a customer who's just made a big purchase from you unless they show intent.

Some credit card companies do a great job with the Engage stage. For individual customers, they go way beyond rewards points and offer low-priced tickets for concerts and other events. American Express has turned itself into a champion for small businesses with its OPEN Forum, a virtual library of small business tips, and its annual Small Business Saturday.

I know a guy who, the day after selling his small business and canceling the AmEx card he had used with it for a decade, realized that he had had 90,000 unused rewards points when he canceled the card. Oops! He called AmEx and explained the situation. They immediately said no problem: he could still cash in the points. That's how you build customer loyalty for the long run.

Beyond retention, you want to turn your customers into champions who will refer and recommend you to potential customers. These are the customers with whom you can create case studies, shoot video testimonials, and source quotes for your website. They'll talk you up without you even knowing about it. Those recommended leads may close at a very high rate—higher than any other marketing channel. They're gold. Outperformers treat all customers like potential advocates.

You should be constantly searching online for those reviewing your products, positively or negatively. YouTube is the second largest search engine behind Google[2]—more than likely, there are both detractors and evangelists for your products there. Reach out to see if there is a way you can work together! Similarly, for Gen Z, Instagram and TikTok are more popular than Google or Bing.[3] Individuals in this generation trust peer-based content more than that served by more traditional search engines. Make sure you know what is being said and who is saying it on these platforms! Potential partnerships abound.

And always remember: the best customer experiences are created through constant communication and partnership with your customers.

UPSELLING CUSTOMERS

Insurance companies often offer bundled policies at discount prices. They may also provide drivers with win-win safe driving discounts and services to B2B customers to help them reduce accidents, fires, and other hazards.

Could you provide personalized recommendations for customers based on their past behavior or type of business (kind of like Amazon's "people who bought this also bought . . ." feature)? Your first-party data on how they first engaged with your company and which products they bought can be critical for this. Think outside the box—the products or services don't necessarily need to be only those you own or control. Are there companies that you could partner with that provide complementary offerings that your customers would find valuable?

Talk to your customers and find out what they would most value. What would white glove service mean to them?

For any subscription business, a critical moment is renewal time. Of course, making renewals automatic unless canceled takes care of that problem. But if people need to actively renew, then make it easy and go through the kind of 45-day or so reminder process that I describe in the case study at the end of this chapter.

Price discounts in general are a bad idea: they weaken your brand and train customers to wait for a sale. The times when they might be a good idea are when you offer higher discounts for longer extension periods or if you are trying to reactivate a customer you know is lost. Do not offer discounts before the average renewal or second order time frame. However, if the average second order time frame is six months and it has been nine months, a discount for a complementary product may help with reactivation. The mistake people make is getting hooked on discounts as the *only* way to get renewals or increase sales.

There are other ways to add value to a customer that do not include strictly discounting. For example, if you know that your average order value is $500, add an incentive to take that order to $600—free shipping, a "freebie" item, etc. You can personalize this offer for individual accounts to move them up in value.

On the other hand, don't make it super hard to cancel, like some software companies that let you buy online but make you call them to cancel. That kind of terrible customer experience will turn around and bite you in the long run. Think of how bad the raps are on some cable companies.

For non-subscription products, cross-selling and upselling are the priorities. Use a prudent mix of value-added messages and sales opportunities to maximize your additional sales.

A metric that you can use for this stage is net dollar retention (NDR): the percentage of revenue retained from your existing customer base from year to year. Ideally, you will be upselling current customers enough so that it will, at a minimum, cover the revenue you lose due to churn. So NDR should be 100% or higher. That will be difficult to achieve with a high churn rate, so you need to be successful at bringing that down as much as possible.

SEGMENTING YOUR CUSTOMERS

You segmented prospects. For optimal results, you need to segment customers, too.

You may segment customers by type, by size and potential purchases, by past purchases, and even by the marketing channels that led them to engage with you in the first place.

You've certainly got high-, middle-, and low-value customers. The most efficient way to increase customer lifetime value is to turn the low into the medium, the medium into the high, and the high into the higher.

Analyze your database to understand the most cross-purchased items by other companies in their segment and recommend them.

Communicate differently with customers depending on their potential lifetime value. Some customers are worth emails and an annual phone call; some may be worth a fancy dinner out with their +1 and more.

And have segments for those who have stopped buying from you. Some companies that send out physical catalogs keep at it so long after the customer has stopped buying from them that they may actually transform once-profitable customers into money losers. Use inexpensive marketing channels, like email marketing, for former customers. Sometimes you just have to acknowledge that the business relationship is over and move on to gaining and growing other accounts.

DOES A LOYALTY PROGRAM MAKE SENSE FOR YOUR COMPANY?

B2B loyalty programs can be tricky. B2C loyalty programs usually benefit individuals; they are personally incentivized to take advantage of them. One extreme example I heard of was a guy who would use connecting flights for business rather than nonstop. The flights took longer, but he could build up more miles that way.

B2B loyalty programs often are focused on solving the business's pain points. But can you make it valuable for the individual, too? To get people to participate, they need to understand why your program is valuable for them.

A useful type of loyalty program for many tech companies is certification. When an individual is certified for a skill and for knowledge of a particular technology, their company can promote that they have X number of certified individuals on staff, and the person has a credential that travels with them.

If you have partners, it's critical to get mindshare from their salespeople. Could you incentivize them with redeemable rewards points based on their level of sales? If companies have President's Clubs, could you have a President's Club for partners? (This also might involve some gamification, such as a leaderboard.)

A problem you may run into is limits on gifts that an employee can receive from a vendor or customer.

But you don't necessarily need a loyalty program. They're not simple to execute well, and you certainly don't want one if people see it as a hassle or don't get value from it. Focusing more on retention and growth may be a better solution.

Byron Sharp says that loyalty programs often just reward the people who would be buying from the company anyway and don't really drive incremental new sales.[4] That may be true for large B2C brands with huge awareness and market share. But a well-thought-out loyalty program can definitely make a difference for smaller companies.

Beware: if you ask customers what they want in a loyalty program they are always going to mention price in the top three—that does not necessarily mean you should discount.

Also, note that once you introduce a program of this type, it is very difficult to cancel or modify it.

Dunkin' Donuts discovered this when it "updated" its popular loyalty program, which kept its customers happy and wired with an endless stream of free coffees. Merely being alive for all sorts of holidays—real and imaginary—won you a free coffee. As did a generous points system. When Dunkin' rolled back these benefits, its most loyal customers felt betrayed, and they lashed out on social media. Many vowed to take their coffee business elsewhere. Then news outlets ran stories about the uproar, dealing out an even bigger brand bruising.[5]

Delta Airlines faced similar backlash over a rolled-back rewards program. In addition to infuriating customers, inviting social media outrage, and tarnishing the brand in the news, the change encouraged proactive customer-poaching from competitors. Smelling fresh meat, Alaska Airlines and JetBlue swooped in with limited-time offers directly targeted at Delta's "Medallion" members. These other airlines offered to match current Delta rewards if frequent flyers defected.[6]

The point is this: loyalty programs are a dangerous game. They must be introduced, structured, and restructured with care. So think twice before you launch one. And if you do launch one, make sure you've got a loyalty program expert on your team.

INTEGRATED CAMPAIGNS FOR RETENTION AND GROWTH

Integrated, multi-channel marketing can be just as valuable in the retention and growth stages as it was in the acquisition and conversion stages.

Now it's easier: you have the customer's email address and their implicit permission to communicate with them. Use it; don't abuse it.

If yours is a subscription business, use the least costly channels—email and digital display ads—to move them to renew. People may respond differently based on their income. A high-income person may renew early to get it out of the way, while a low-income person may put it off until the last minute. For them, nothing motivates like a deadline. Only when you're getting down to the wire should you switch to more expensive channels like one-to-one calls and physical mail.

You can also use those email addresses to target customers using programmatic ads and social media ads. These can be a great, inexpensive way to keep your upsell/cross-sell offerings in front of them.

If you have a customer portal or community, you can remarket to the people who are using them.

For items with deadlines like renewals, use the time decay attribution model to understand how your different channels contribute to success. How much you spend on promoting these add-ons will depend on their value.

CASE STUDY—MAKE NEW FRIENDS, BUT KEEP THE OLD

To sell insurance to professionals in the beauty field, including hair stylists, estheticians, and cosmetologists, we created the Elite Beauty Society (www.elitebeautysociety.com). Through it, we offered a variety of liability and other policies for less than $200 per year (slightly more if they paid monthly).

In addition to the insurance, customers receive membership benefits such as ebooks, guides, waivers, intake forms, surveys, and partnerships that provide them with discounted or free member benefits. We think of it as a "business in a box." These value-adds ensure the brand is in constant contact with our customers with a message other than those related to renewal. This is key as it creates a stronger bond with the brand and creates a stickier customer base.

Of course, a high retention rate is critical to success. That, and upsells and partner sales, is how we can get the customer lifetime up and justify spending more on customer acquisition. So, as we approach the customer renewal date, we implemented planned sets of messages:

- Ongoing social media efforts beginning 45 days before expiration
- 45-day letter (This is required because insurance is a regulated industry. But these mailers are very expensive. So if they weren't required, we wouldn't send them so early.)
- 45-day email
- 30-day email
- 15-day email
- 15-day postcard

- 5-day phone call

- 1-day email

Hello **Sara**,

Your current insurance policy expires on 6/10/2022 12:00:00 AM, which is 15 days from now.

Elite Beauty Society is the #1 insurance provider for thousands of beauty professionals across the U.S. With over 5- star, independent customer reviews and A+ rated coverage, we are confident we can continue to protect your career better than ever.

Check out what EBS customer, Cynthia, has to say:

CY	Cynthia
	✎ 1 review ⊚ US

★★★★★ ✔ Verified   Feb 1, 2022

It's nice to know you can have one...

It's nice to know you can have one company for tons of resources and support. I'm so happy and pleased with this company! I would recommend them to anyone!

👍 Useful   ⤳ Share   ⚐

Don't miss out on another year of career protection and growth. **Click below to renew your policy and receive instant coverage for the next year.**

Renew Now

Beauty **Insurance+**

It's Time To Renew!
Your liability insurance with Beauty Insurance Plus is expiring soon.

We are dedicated to protecting you against any accidents that may happen in the salon. From allergic reactions to cuts or burns, and even slip and fall, we are here to make sure your career is protected at every stage of your career.

★★★★★ Trustpilot
It's so nice to know I'm covered if something unexpected happens. I've been in the business for 49 years!

Rosemary, BIP Customer

Membership Highlights

- $3 Million in Professional and General Liability Insurance
- $2 Million in Product Liability Insurance
- Over $700 in Exclusive Industry and Lifestyle Discounts
- Mobile Coverage; You're Protected Wherever You Practice

If they don't renew by their deadline, we have a post-renewal cadence, too, which includes an email and call on their renewal date. They then are asked to participate in a (non-renewers) survey, so we can better understand why people don't renew, and we can improve our offering so that others will in the future. Finally, they do continue to receive monthly, post-expiration emails and social media promotions.

Through this effort, we're able to achieve a renewal rate of 59%. That would be poor for SaaS, but it is well above average in this market where many people are typically only in business for a year or two. When normalized for industry churn, the renewal rate was 89%.

FIVE-TACTIC FUNNELING

We've now seen how the Five-Tactic Marketing Framework plays out across every stage of the funnel. Here again, in post-conversion, we saw that no single tactic has the unilateral power to create an outperforming campaign. It's the combination of all five tactics, operating in unison, that transforms our work.

We build brand value with deeply considered customer experiences (tactic #1). We upsell, cross-sell, and promote renewals through the very same performance marketing techniques that won over our customers in the first place (also tactic #1). We roll out all of these efforts via integrated campaigns—spanning all appropriate channels and speaking directly to the unique needs of our customers (tactics #3 and #4). All of this ultimately enhances our customer lifetime value, which radically boosts the marketing dollars available across the rest of our Lifetime Value Framework (tactic #2). And, as we'll see in just a moment, every element of these post-conversion efforts can be dramatically enhanced with the use of artificial intelligence (tactic #5).

After we cover AI's role in all this, we'll be moving into this book's conclusion, where we'll take stock of what we've learned so far and what it takes to implement all of it. But before we do, I want to take a moment to highlight the incredible simplicity of what we discovered here in Part II.

For all the technicalities, for all the if-then considerations, for all the fine-tuning and optimizing, it comes down to this: breaking past sales plateaus, ensuring profitability, and growing our businesses requires no secret sauce. No hacks. No arcane strategies. It requires only that we collect the tools all around us—the tools that every marketer has access to—and deploy them in concert.

The mistake that's made all too often is merely this: we develop siloed expertise or rely on one-tactic strategies. Merely by combining all the tools at our disposal, we can transform our futures and the futures of our companies.

AI USE CASES: CUSTOMER RETENTION AND UPSELL ENABLED BY AI

Creation
Personalization

As we've seen before, AI adds extraordinary new personalization capabilities to your marketing toolkit. The value of those capabilities only grows post-funnel, when customers are hungriest for that personal touch. Ultimately, personalized messaging, design, and recommendations are important both for deepening customer relationships and for identifying the most promising upsell/cross-sell/renewal opportunities.

Product Development

As we've seen before, one of AI's greatest strengths is that it can put lots of apparently unrelated data in conversation, crunch all the numbers, perform a deep analysis, and make recommendations accordingly. Product development is another great use case. AI tools can assess purchase behaviors in conjunction with other data sets in order to recommend concepts for new products or product bundles. For example, the AI might identify that buyers of Widget A often call customer service in need of an adapter for Widget B; it would then suggest that a product bundle is in order.

Operation

Customer Scoring/Segmentation

Throughout this book, we've noted that one of the best ways to boost your marketing budget is to boost your post-funnel customer lifetime value. That makes post-funnel scoring and segmentation just as important now as it was during acquisition and conversion. AIs use purchase history and other criteria to score and segment your current customers, faster and in more depth than humans can. Ultimately, AI tools may make surprising discoveries—like perhaps that big spenders generate little value for your business, while your most valuable customers make relatively small purchases more frequently over a greater period of time.

Marketing Automation

Marketing automation is as powerful post-funnel as it was during conversion. And, like in conversion, you can use these AI tools both for deployment and for personalization. Namely, you can use them to manage and fine-tune upsell/cross-sell/renewal campaigns in real time, monitoring and responding to incoming engagement and sales figures. And you can also use these tools to tailor and time overtures to individual customers. (More on the latter application follows.)

Product Recommendation

A sub-type of personalization. Have an AI study individual customers' purchase history, browsing history, and other data in order to identify other products that may interest them. Then present those cross-sell/upsell product recommendations on your website, in emails, in targeted ads, and even during sales calls.

Content Recommendation

The same principle as earlier, but for content. Your AI tools will study customer behavior, purchases, and other indicators, and then make their recommendations. This is a great way to ensure that the right content is getting to the right customers—those who will value it most.

Customer Service

Quality customer service is one of the most powerful predictors of customer lifetime value. Get it right, and you foster loyalty. Get it wrong, and you foster resentment. This is especially important post-conversion, when returns, exchanges, and other kinds of customer support become one of the primary channels of engagement. So this is where you'll most want to invest in customer service AI, ensuring speed and accuracy in response to customer queries. As noted before, these tools can be implemented both externally (with customer-facing chatbots) and internally (with chatbots that help your support team).

Optimization

Performance Analysis

Real-time performance analysis is as important here as it was during acquisition and conversion. Use AI tools to monitor and analyze interactions, sentiment, and upsell/cross-sell/renewal success metrics. Then fine-tune your post-conversion campaigns in response to those insights.

Financial Assessment

The math of the Lifetime Value Framework all hinges on customer lifetime value, which, in turn, hinges on the performance of upsell, cross-sell, and renewal efforts. That's why you'll want to deploy number-crunching AI tools here to constantly monitor changes to lifetime value and assess how those changes are cascading down through the Lifetime Value Framework. These tools will help you determine how you're performing and what needs to change.

CONCLUSION:
PUTTING IT ALL TOGETHER

A rising tide lifts all boats. Only when the tide goes out do you discover who's been swimming naked.

—WARREN BUFFETT

I developed the Five-Tactic Marketing Framework through constant experimentation at Direct to Policyholder (DTPH), a performance marketing firm I created for selling insurance and other products to a range of small business professionals. Before that, I had worked as a business consultant for IBM based in Hong Kong, working with clients like Ralph Lauren and Cathay Pacific. At IBM, I specialized in web analytics and e-commerce implementations. My time there taught me the "dos and don'ts" of digital marketing and sales—lessons that would ultimately lay the groundwork for DTPH's growth and success.

DTPH was one of several companies seeking to disrupt the insurance industry. Traditionally, insurance has been sold by agents. However, we understood that there are types of insurance that are too low-cost to support the manual, agent-centric approach, but that could be profitable if the sale could be automated and policies sold in large enough numbers.

Our competitors were virtually all venture-backed and, like many VC-backed firms, were more focused on growth than profitability. As a family-owned business, we did not have that option (or luxury). And so, we had to figure out how to squeeze as much profit as possible from our operation. The result was the five-tactic approach that you've read about here.

To be successful, we developed proprietary e-commerce technology and brand-specific integrated marketing programs. And we developed our own algorithm to identify new verticals to expand into based on such factors as total addressable market (TAM), average cost per click in paid search, keyword search volume, and others. We entered over 15 markets in 6 years and in less than 18 months achieved top positions in *all of them.* And we weren't doing this on the cheap: we provided a high-value product with a normalized annual retention rate of 80%.

Despite the success of our approach, many of our competitors continued to raise funds in the frothy VC climate of the late teens and early 2020s. However, that all changed in 2022 when rising interest rates ended the days of free money. (In Q3, 2022, VC investments in all industries dropped 53% YOY.)[2] And suddenly the words of Warren Buffett quoted earlier rang true once again.

These were my key lessons.

As noted in Chapter 1, brand and performance marketing make up the first two parts of our framework—and they are strongest when deployed in conversation with one another.

Building a strong brand that is paired with performance marketing is vital to long-term success. Having a great customer experience is an indispensable part of that strong brand. Creating excess share of voice—via many marketing channels—will grow your market share. This includes messaging with a strong emotional component; it will allow you to sell based on something other than price or rate. For DTPH, the emotional component was unique for each market. It included industry-specific content and imagery based on extensive research.

- ✓ Develop a great customer experience (using the Five Es).

- ✓ Market extensively so that you have excess share of voice.

- ✓ Include strong emotional messages to build mental availability.

- ✓ Deploy a multi-channel program across four to six channels, using performance marketing to then close the deal.

In Chapter 2, I introduced the second tactic of SMB marketing: the Lifetime Value Framework (LVF). This is a method to maximize your multi-channel performance marketing profits. Will you be driven by the opportunity for success or limited by an arbitrary budget?

✓ Eschew the budget-limited approach and seek to maximize your profits.

✓ Base your multi-channel approach on Customer Lifetime Value (CLV) with these metrics for each stage:

    › Acquisition: cost per lead (CPM and CPL)

    › Conversion: cost per acquisition (CPA)

    › Customer retention and upsell: increasing CLV

✓ Avoid analysis paralysis, define your stage goals as well as possible with available data, and make course corrections as you learn more.

In Chapter 3, I talked about how critical customer understanding is to the development of successful multi-channel marketing. This was the first step toward establishing our third tactic: understanding your customer.

✓ Overperform by outworking your competitors when it comes to researching your market and understanding your customers.

✓ Recognize the importance of the three types of data, and—as third-party cookies disappear—especially your first-party data.

✓ Spend time developing a qualitative understanding of your customers: what are their emotional drivers?

✓ Develop personas and segments to focus your marketing programs.

In Chapter 4, we filled out the fourth tactic, learning to develop and execute integrated, multi-channel programs.

✓ Multi-channel marketing programs have a far greater impact than single-channel programs.

✓ Start by establishing your North Star: the goals that you'll use to measure success.

✓ In multi-channel campaigns, the critical success factors are:

> Targeting 40%

> Offers 40%

> Creative, etc. 20%

✓ Develop a media plan based on the preferences and behavior of the market you're in; you may want to use a media planner to help develop this.

✓ Use the vast amounts of data provided by digital marketing tools, and increasingly from traditional channels, to optimize your campaigns.

✓ Create a consistent cross-channel customer experience.

Then came Part II of the book, where we applied the Five-Tactic Marketing Framework to each stage of the funnel.

In Chapter 5, we explored the acquisition stage, where you put to use what you've learned about your customers and their emotional drivers and begin to implement the program that you've planned.

✓ Cost per thousand (CPM) and Cost per lead (CPL) are the primary LVF metrics for this stage.

✓ This is the trickiest stage because you're dealing with three different levels of intent.

✓ Level of intent will drive everything from channel selection to messaging to offers.

✓ If you already operate a successful marketing program that has C-suite confidence, you can undertake brand-building campaigns whose primary metric is impressions; but if you need to first build their confidence, you should focus on campaigns that quickly drive sales first.

✓ In the long run, organic content may be your most profitable channel, but it can take two to three years or more to get significant results from it.

✓ Decide whether to gate a particular piece of content based on its value: only gate your most valuable pieces.

✓ Constantly be testing and working to improve your results.

In Chapter 6, I discussed the critical conversion stage. This is where you close the deal. From a business point of view, nothing else matters.

✓ Cost per acquisition (CPA) is the primary LVF metric for this stage.

✓ Determining allowable CPA may be complicated by a complex product mix and multiple customer segments.

✓ Once again, demonstrated intent will go far in determining the messages and offers you make to a particular account.

  › Low-intent accounts will be nurtured.

  › Medium-intent accounts will begin to receive product information and closing messages.

  › High-intent accounts, such as ones with an abandoned shopping cart, will be targeted with a full-court press of closing strategies.

✓ Conversion rate optimization can easily improve your results by 50–100%, and sometimes even more.

✓ Test your user experience, including user interfaces, to make sure that they are as easy and convenient as possible.

✓ You may be tempted to use last click attribution in this stage, but remember that virtually all sales actually had many interactions with your company before the sale, so a model like time decay may be more accurate.

In Chapter 7, we went over the final stage—customer retention and upsell—in which you work to increase customer lifetime value (CLV). By doing so, you not only increase profits but also have more latitude for generating future leads and sales.

✓ In this stage, the primary LVF metric is CLV.

✓ Of the Five Es of Customer Experience, Enter, Engage, and Extend are all relevant.

✓ Constantly provide value and occasionally make upsell offers.

✓ For a renewal business, use a cross-channel cadence of messages to maximize renewals.

✓ Segment your customers and work to move low-value customers to middle and middle to high.

✓ Loyalty programs are complicated, and you may have greater success if you focus more on renewals and upsells.

And finally, throughout the book, we've returned again and again to the fifth tactic, exploring how AI tools dramatically expand and enhance our capabilities—across the other tactics, across the entire funnel, and across three major domains: creation, operation, and optimization.

✓ Creation: Use AI tools to ideate both strategically and creatively.

Then use them again to execute on creative direction, generating text, art, video, code, web-based assets, and other media.

✓ Operation: Build an AI operations "team" to roll out, monitor, maintain, run, and recalibrate your campaigns. To name just a few examples, AIs can help you segment customers, score leads, analyze sentiment, tailor recommendations, and even run customer service operations.

✓ Optimization: Finally, bring in AI tools to optimize financial performance, determining LVF allowables, calculating projections, comparing attribution models, analyzing performance, visualizing data, and testing various pricing schemes.

That's a lot.

This isn't easy. It's complicated, and it means that you'll have to outwork the competition. But as Tom Hanks's character says in *A League of Their Own*, "It's supposed to be hard. If it wasn't hard, everyone would do it."[2]

Remember what I said at the beginning of this Conclusion: using the Five-Tactic Marketing Framework, in less than 18 months we rose to top positions in every market we entered.

This approach has done great things for my career and the companies that I've worked for. Taking advantage of what I've learned, you can outmarket your competitors too.

I HOPE YOU ENJOYED THE BOOK!
PLEASE LEAVE A REVIEW!

If you've found *Outmarket the Competition* helpful, I would greatly appreciate it if you could take a moment to leave a review on Amazon.

Your feedback helps other readers discover the book and supports me in continuing to provide valuable content.

Just scan the QR code below to leave your review.

**FAST
COMPANY**
Press

TOOLS AND RESOURCES

Tools and resources are constantly evolving. To stay ahead of the curve and ensure you're leveraging the latest advancements, it's crucial to have the newest tools at hand.

That's why I've created a dedicated section on my website where you can access a curated list of the most current and effective tools and resources by category.

Simply scan the QR code below to explore:

Link address: https://nickdoyle.com/resources

FAST
COMPANY
Press

NOTES

CHAPTER 1

1. Claude Hopkins, *Scientific Advertising* (1923), 53.

2. Scott Brinker, "Marketing Technology Landscape 2022," Chief Martech, May 3, 2022, https://chiefmartec.com/2022/05/marketing-technology-landscape-2022-search-9932-solutions-on-martechmap-com.

3. Byron Sharp, *How Brands Grow: What Marketers Don't Know* (Oxford, England: Oxford University Press, 2010).

4. Matthew Valentine, "Ehrenberg-Bass: 95% of B2B Buyers Are Not in the Market for Your Products," *MarketingWeek,* July 15, 2021, https://www.marketingweek.com/ehrenberg-bass-linkedin-b2b-buyers.

5. Les Binet and Peter Field, *The Long and the Short of It* (The Institute of Practitioners in Advertising, 2013), and "The 5 Principles of Growth in B2B Marketing," The B2B Institute by LinkedIn, 2019, https://business.linkedin.com/marketing-solutions/b2b-institute/marketing-as-growth.

6. Mark Ritson, "Ritson on Marketing Effectiveness," *News Media Works*, 2019, YouTube, https://www.youtube.com/watch?v=vlFOkP2Mh9c&t.

7. Paul Dyson, "Top 10 Drivers of Advertising Profitability," WARC, September 2014, https://docplayer.net/35570251-Top-10-drivers-of-advertising-profitability.html.

8. Jenni Romaniuk, *Building Distinctive Brand Assets* (Oxford, England: Oxford University Press, 2018).

9. LinkedIn's The B2B Institute, https://business.linkedin.com/marketing-solutions/b2b-institute.

10. "Discover the Kantar BrandZ Most Valuable Global Brands," Kantar, 2023, https://www.kantar.com/campaigns/brandz/global.

11. See, for example, Dyson, "Top 10 Drivers," which ranked market share as the #1 multiplier of advertising ROI.

12. Martin Kihn, "How to Measure the Impact of Brand Advertising," Gartner, May 29, 2018, https://blogs.gartner.com/martin-kihn/how-to-measure-the-impact-of-brand-advertising.

13. Sharp, *How Brands Grow*.

14. Robert Johnson, "Ten Myths of B2B Buyers #7: B2B Buyers Respond to 'Steak so' Forget the 'Sizzle,'" LinkedIn Newsletters, June 23, 2016, https://www.linkedin.com/pulse/ten-myths-b2b-buyers-7-respond-steak-so-forget-sizzle-bob-johnson.

15. Scott Magids, Alan Zorfas, and Daniel Leemon, "The New Science of Customer Emotions," *Harvard Business Review*, November 2015, https://hbr.org/2015/11/the-new-science-of-customer-emotions.

16. E. Jerome McCarthy, *Basic Marketing: A Managerial Approach* (New York: Irwin, 1964).

17. Leonard M. Lodish and Carl F. Mela, "If Brands Are Built Over Years, Why Are They Managed Over Quarters?," *Harvard Business Review*, July–August 2007, https://hbr.org/2007/07/if-brands-are-built-over-years-why-are-they-managed-over-quarters.

18. Sarah Vizard, "Adidas: We Over-Invested in Digital Advertising," *MarketingWeek*, October 17, 2019, https://www.marketingweek.com/adidas-marketing-effectiveness.

19. Daniel Kahneman, *Thinking Fast and Slow* (New York: Farrar, Straus and Giroux, 2011). On Amazon, it has an astonishing 39,770+ ratings with an average of 4.6 out of 5. My mention of those numbers is a form of social proof, another emotional motivator.

20. Kahneman, *Thinking Fast and Slow*.

21. Dyson, "Top 10 Drivers."

22. Johnson, "Ten Myths of B2B Buyers #7."

23. Roger L. Martin, Jann Schwarz, and Mimi Turner, "The Right Way to Build Your Brand," *Harvard Business Review*, January–February 2024, https://hbr.org/2024/01/the-right-way-to-build-your-brand#:~:text=As%20we%27ll%20explain%2C%20the,latter%20creates%20greater%20name%20awareness.

24. Martin, Schwarz, and Turner, "The Right Way to Build Your Brand."

25. "Overview: HubSpot," SpyFu, https://www.spyfu.com/keyword/overview?query=hubspot.

26. Tony Silber, "Harvard Business Review Pivots to a Digital-First Marketing Model," *Forbes*, June 29, 2018, https://www.forbes.com/sites/

tonysilber/2018/06/29/harvard-business-review-pivots-to-a-digital-first-marketing-model.

27. Silber, "Harvard Business Review Pivots."

28. How good is Salesforce at brand marketing? LinkedIn's B2B Institute's Head of Development, Peter Weinberg, wrote, "For five years, we here at The B2B Institute have been trying to make the case for brand building in B2B. We've conducted empirical research on the benefits of brand with leading experts like Les Binet and Peter Field. We have traveled to the ends of the earth (i.e., Australia) to share that research with our clients. But if you want to convince someone to do something, research will only get you so far—what you really need are examples. Luckily, the universe gave us Salesforce. Whenever I am asked 'who is doing everything right' in B2B, my answer is always the same: Salesforce. As far as I'm concerned, Salesforce is the best B2B marketing organization in the world." Peter Weinberg, "The Importance of B2B Brand Building," *LinkedIn Ads Blog*, April 20, 2021, https://www.linkedin.com/business/marketing/blog/brand/the-importance-of-b2b-brand-building.

29. "Top Trends from the CMO Survey," Deloitte, https://www2.deloitte.com/us/en/pages/chief-marketing-officer/articles/cmo-survey.html.

30. Louis Gudema, *Bullseye Marketing* (Wedgewood Press, 2018).

CHAPTER 2

1. Claude Hopkins, *Scientific Advertising* (1923), 55.

2. Stefan Tornquist, "2019 Marketing Operations Maturity Benchmarking," Econsultancy, June 2019, https://econsultancy.com/reports/2019-marketing-operations-maturity-benchmarking/.

3. Byron Sharp, *How Brands Grow: What Marketers Don't Know* (Oxford, England: Oxford University Press, 2010).

4. Tzvika Barenholz, "The Trouble with Green Dashboards," *Product Coalition*, September 4, 2020, https://productcoalition.com/the-trouble-with-green-dashboards-6921a6a9a0b2.

5. Daniel Slater, "Elements of Amazon's Day 1 Culture," AWS Executive Insights, https://aws.amazon.com/executive-insights/content/how-amazon-defines-and-operationalizes-a-day-1-culture/.

6. Avinash Kaushik, *Occam's Razor* (blog), https://www.kaushik.net/avinash.

7. Brent Gleeson, "9 Navy SEAL Sayings That Will Improve Your Organization's Ability to Lead Change," *Forbes*, https://www.forbes.com/

sites/brentgleeson/2018/07/23/9-navy-seal-sayings-that-will-improve-your-organizations-ability-to-lead-change/#734763ce64d4.

8. Remember that Binet & Field said that brand marketing campaigns don't hit maximum effectiveness for two to three years. Once they hit that peak performance, though, they may continue to deliver results at that level for years. Nike's "Just Do It" and Progressive Insurance's "Flo" campaigns are two current examples of successful long-term campaigns. Many marketing campaigns fail, though, simply because the company leadership didn't have the patience to give them the time to succeed.

9. Emad Hasan, "What Should Your CLV to CAC Ratio Be?," Retina.ai, https://retina.ai/blog/ufaqs/what-should-your-clv-to-cac-ratio-be. CAC is determined with this formula: (sales + marketing)/number of new customers = CAC.

10. David Ogilvy, *Ogilvy on Advertising* (New York: Vintage Books, 1985), 20.

CHAPTER 3

1. David Ogilvy, *Ogilvy on Advertising* (New York: Vintage Books, 1985).

2. Jean B. McGuire, Barclay E. James, and Andrew Papadopoulos, "Do Your Findings Depend on Your Data(base)?," *Journal of International Management* 22, no. 2 (June 2016): 186–206, https://www.sciencedirect.com/science/article/abs/pii/S1075425316300795. This "database effect" is even stronger in emerging markets.

3. You may be limited in the use of all data by such laws as the California Consumer Privacy Act (CCPA) and the EU's GDPR. You're also limited, of course, by your own publicly available privacy policy and related policies.

4. David Ogilvy, *Confessions of an Advertising Man* (Harpenden, UK: Southbank Publishing, 2012).

5. "The Market Segmentation Playbook," Demandbase, 2022, p 12, https://www.demandbase.com/resources/ebook/market-segmentation-playbook.

6. Charles Duhigg, "How Companies Learn Your Secrets," *New York Times Magazine*, February 16, 2012, https://www.nytimes.com/2012/02/19/magazine/shopping-habits.html.

7. "Gartner Survey Shows Brands Risk Losing 38 Percent of Customers Because of Poor Marketing Personalization Efforts," Gartner, March 11, 2012, https://www.gartner.com/en/newsroom/press-releases/2019-03-11-gartner-survey-shows-brands-risk-losing-38-percent-of

CHAPTER 4

1. Dave Lance, "Bull's-Eye Squarely on Hawks' Backs," *Dayton Daily News,* February 25, 2004.

2. Public Papers of the Presidents of the United States, Dwight D. Eisenhower, 1957, Containing the Public Messages, Speeches, and Statements of the President, Remarks at the National Defense Executive Reserve Conference, November 14, 1957, Published by the Federal Register Division, National Archives and Records Service, General Services Administration, Washington D.C. (HathiTrust Full View), https://babel.hathitrust.org/cgi/pt?id=miua.4728417.1957.001&seq=858.

3. Michel Laroche, Isar Kiani, Nectarios Economakis, and Marie-Odile Richard, "Effects of Multi-Channel Marketing on Consumers' Online Search Behavior: The Power of Multiple Points of Connection," *Journal of Advertising Research,* 53, no. 4 (December 2013): 431–443, https://www.journalofadvertisingresearch.com/content/53/4/431.

4. Brent Adamson, "Traditional B2B Sales and Marketing Are Becoming Obsolete," *Harvard Business Review,* February 1, 2022, https://hbr.org/2022/02/traditional-b2b-sales-and-marketing-are-becoming-obsolete.

5. Andrew Noble, James Anderson, and Sam Thakarar, "Three Rules for Building the Modern Retail Organization," Bain & Company, June 17, 2015, https://www.bain.com/insights/three-rules-for-building-the-modern-retail-organization.

6. Laroche, Kiani, Economakis, and Richard, "Effects of Multi-Chanel Marketing."

7. Jacqueline Zote, "12 Essential Twitter stats to guide your strategy," Sprout Social, originally published March 10, 2022, https://web.archive.org/web/20210312160025/https://sproutsocial.com/insights/twitter-statistics/.

8. Meltem Odabas, "8 Facts about Americans and Twitter," Pew Research Center, May 5, 2022, https://www.pewresearch.org/fact-tank/2022/05/05/10-facts-about-americans-and-twitter. This was written just as Elon Musk was taking over Twitter (now "X"); these numbers may have changed significantly since then.

9. Brian Dean, "We Analyzed 4 Million Google Search Results," Backlinko, May 28, 2023, https://backlinko.com/google-ctr-stats.

10. In Chapter 1, I mentioned Louis Gudema's *Bullseye Marketing.* He provides an excellent framework for choosing and launching channels based on how affordable and fast they are to perform.

11. Al DiCroce, "3 Reasons Why Direct Mail Is Making a Comeback," Trib Total Media, October 15, 2020, https://mediakit.triblive.com/blog/3-reasons-why-direct-mail-marketing-is-making-a-comeback.

12. Avinash Kaushik, *Occam's Razor* (blog), https://www.kaushik.net/avinash/?s= data+puking.

13. Brendan Coyne, "Prof. Byron Sharp Skewers Binet & Field's 60:40 Rule," Mi3, August 23, 2022, https://www.mi-3.com.au/23-08-2022/byron-sharp-skewers-binet-and-fields-6040-rule-smashes-attention-metrics-bvod-ad?s=03.

14. "How to Improve the Customer Experience," McKinsey & Company, March 6, 2022, https://www.mckinsey.com/featured-insights/themes/how-to-improve-the-customer-experience. This page is an overview of McKinsey insights on CX with links to 11 pieces from them on the topic.

15. Brent Schlender and Rick Tetzeli, *Becoming Steve Jobs* (New York: Crown Business, 2015), 349.

16. "Our Core Values," Patagonia, https://www.patagonia.com/core-values.

17. "Ironclad Guarantee," Patagonia, https://help.patagonia.com/s/article/Ironclad-Guarantee.

18. As of September 1, 2022, "HubSpot," CompaniesMarketCap, https://companiesmarketcap.com/hubspot/revenue/#:~:text=According%20to%20 HubSpot's%20latest%20financial,sale%20of%20goods%20or%20services.

19. "Total Number of Websites," Internet Live Stats, https://www.internetlivestats.com/total-number-of-websites.

20. Rand Fishkin, "The Future of SEO Has Never Been Clearer (Nor More Ignored)," *SparkToro* (blog), August 1, 2018, https://sparktoro.com/blog/the-future-of-seo-has-never-been-clearer-nor-more-ignored.

21. Thomas J. Steenburgh, Jill Avery, and Naseem Ashraf Dahod, "HubSpot: Inbound Marketing and Web 2.0," *Harvard Business School*, originally published 2009, revised January 24, 2011, https://www.hbs.edu/faculty/Pages/item.aspx?num=37327.

22. "HubSpot," CrunchBase, https://www.crunchbase.com/organization/hubspot/company_financials.

23. Louis Gudema, "Can HubSpot Afford to Do Inbound Marketing Anymore? Can You?" Revenue & Associates, September 18, 2017, https://revenueassociates.biz/hubspot-afford-inbound-marketing-customer-acquisition-cost-2. At that point, HubSpot stopped including CAC in its annual reports; maybe it had gotten too embarrassing.

24. "2014 Year in Review," HubSpot, 9, https://www.hubspot.com/2014-year-in-review.

25. beYogi, https://beyogi.com.

CHAPTER 5

1. John Caples, *Tested Advertising Methods* (New Jersey: Prentice Hall, 1997).

2. Tim Soulo, "How Long Does It Take to Rank in Google?," *Ahrefs* (blog), February 7, 2017, https://ahrefs.com/blog/how-long-does-it-take-to-rank.

3. Robert Rose, "To Gate or Not to Gate? Is That Really the Question?," Content Marketing Institute, July 22, 2020, https://contentmarketinginstitute.com/articles/gated-content-audience-journey.

4. John Becker, "Should You Still Gate Your Content in 2024?," ImpactPlus, October 5, 2023, https://www.impactplus.com/blog/should-you-still-gate-your-inbound-content-in-2020.

5. Larry Kim, "What's a Good Conversion Rate? (It's Higher Than You Think)," *WordStream* (blog), updated November 13, 2023, https://www.wordstream.com/blog/ws/2014/03/17/what-is-a-good-conversion-rate.

6. Katie Holmes, "Updated 2023: Average Conversion Rate by Industry and Marketing Source," Ruler Analytics, February 3, 2023, https://web.archive.org/web/20230326002502/https://www.ruleranalytics.com/blog/insight/conversion-rate-by-industry/.

7. Becker, "Should You Still Gate."

8. Louis Gudema, "Don't be Overly Driven by Data," ModernMSP, March 30, 2022, https://web.archive.org/web/20221203052433/https://modernmsp.io/msps-dont-be-overly-driven-by-data/.

9. ZoomInfo, "Marketing Attribution: The Beginner's Guide for B2B," The Pipeline, updated December 22, 2023, https://pipeline.zoominfo.com/marketing/b2b-marketing-attribution-modeling.

10. Avinash Kaushik, "TMAI #327: Attribution Modeling? Stop," *The Marketing <> Analytics Intersect*, September 22, 2022, https://tmai.avinashkaushik.com/web-version?ep=1&lc=28ab81b5-bfda-11ea-a3d0-06b4694bee2a&p=cd8465b8-3a25-11ed-9a32-0241b9615763&pt=campaign&t=1669317537&s=081672283abdd54ce28a77a5b33ef208e38adb6c90d0255f03eda2ca241625e8.

11. Scott Rheinlander, "Everything You Wanted to Know About Marketing Attribution Models (but Were Afraid to Ask)," Salesforce, *360 Blog*, April 19, 2019, https://www.salesforce.com/blog/what-is-marketing-attribution-model.

12. In this case, consolidating the websites made sense. It doesn't always. For example, when Zillow bought Realtor.com they chose to keep their brands and sites separate so they could retain the #1 and #2 placements on most property-related search results.

CHAPTER 6

1. Peter Drucker, *The Practice of Management* reissue (New York: Harper Business, 2006).

2. Daniel Kahneman, *Thinking Fast and Slow* (New York: Farrar, Straus and Giroux, 2011).

3. "Sensational Software, Sensible Price," Zoho, accessed October 2022, https://www.zoho.com/crm/zohocrm-pricing.html.

4. Robert Cialdini, *Influence* (New York: Harper Business, 1984).

5. Nancy Harhut, *Using Behavioral Science in Marketing* (New York: Kogan Page, 2022).

6. Steve Kru, *Don't Make Me Think* (2000) and Claude Hopkins, *Scientific Advertising* (1923). These are two other books I find very valuable. Technology may change, but people don't; the direct response and CRO techniques that worked 10, 20, 50, or even 100 years ago are likely to still work for you.

7. Harhut, *Using Behavioral Science.*

8. Prisync, "Decoy Pricing: Influence Sales to the Right Direction," Prisync, May 10, 2019, https://prisync.com/blog/decoy-pricing.

9. The insights into the development of the Apple store are from Brent Schlender and Rick Tetzeli, *Becoming Steve Jobs* (New York: Crown Business, 2015), 278–281.

10. Tony Hsieh, "How I Did It: Zappos's CEO on Going to Extremes for Customers," *Harvard Business Review,* July–August 2010, https://hbr.org/2010/07/how-i-did-it-zapposs-ceo-on-going-to-extremes-for-customers.

11. "Amazon Leadership Principles," Amazon, https://www.aboutamazon.com/about-us/leadership-principles.

CHAPTER 7

1. Lester Wunderman, *Being Direct* (New York: Random House, 1996).

2. "YouTube the Second Largest Search Engine," Mushroom Networks, https://visual.ly/community/Infographics/social-media/youtube-2nd-largest-search-engine.

3. Kalley Huang, "For Gen Z, TikTok Is the New Search Engine," *New York Times*, September 16, 2022, https://www.nytimes.com/2022/09/16/technology/gen-z-tiktok-search-engine.html.

4. Byron Sharp, *How Brands Grow: What Marketers Don't Know* (Oxford, England: Oxford University Press, 2010).

5. Angela Yang, "Dunkin' Changed Its Rewards Program. Devotees of the Coffee Brand Are Expressing Their Outrage on Reddit," *NBC News*, October 12, 2022, https://www.nbcnews.com/business/dunkin-donuts-new-rewards-program-reddit-backlash-rcna50940# and Amy Laskowski, "Why Dunkin's Revamped Rewards Program Has Angered So Many Customers," *BU Today*, October 31, 2022, https://www.bu.edu/articles/2022/why-dunkins-rewards-program-angered-people/.

6. "Delta Is Returning to the Gate to Tweak Unpopular Changes in Its Frequent-Flyer Program," Associated Press, September 27, 2023, https://apnews.com/article/delta-loyalty-program-frequent-flyers-24d9620b38fd6493e6b85d52b95bf7f1?utm_campaign=mb&utm_medium=newsletter&utm_source=morning_brew.

CONCLUSION

1. Gené Teare, "Global VC Pullback Is Dramatic in Q3 2022," Crunchbase, October 6, 2022, https://news.crunchbase.com/venture/global-vc-funding-pullback-q3-2022-monthly-recap.

2. Dir. Penny Marshall, *A League of Their Own*, Columbia Pictures, 1992.

INDEX

ABOUT THE AUTHOR

NICK DOYLE is a successful entrepreneur with proven performance in building e-commerce-based brands. His career began at IBM Global Services in Hong Kong, where he consulted on web analytics and e-commerce for global brands like Ralph Lauren and Cathay Pacific. That work led him to Direct to Policyholder, an e-commerce technology and marketing firm with more than twenty discrete brands, where he served as Managing Director of Marketing and E-commerce, then COO, before assuming the CEO role. The successful acquisition of Direct to Policyholder led to his most recent role as Area President for Arthur J. Gallagher (NYSE: AJG), a Fortune 300 company and one of the largest insurance brokers worldwide. Throughout his career, Doyle has profitably acquired over a million unique customers.

Doyle has formally studied AI and machine learning at Google, Maven, and Singularity University. He is a member of the Young Presidents' Organization, as well as various angel investing groups.

When not thinking about e-commerce, he enjoys spending time with his wife, Kristin, and son, Theodore.